SAP® Essentials

Expert SAP knowledge for your day-to-day work

Whether you wish to expand your SAP knowledge, deepen it, or master a use case, SAP Essentials provide you with targeted expert knowledge that helps support you in your day-to-day work. To the point, detailed, and ready to use.

SAP PRESS is a joint initiative of SAP and Galileo Press. The know-how offered by SAP specialists combined with the expertise of the Galileo Press publishing house offers the reader expert books in the field. SAP PRESS features first-hand information and expert advice, and provides useful skills for professional decision-making.

SAP PRESS offers a variety of books on technical and business related topics for the SAP user. For further information, please visit our website: *www.sap-press.com.*

Daniel Knapp
SAP NetWeaver BI 7.0 Migration Guide
2008, 180 pp.
978-1-59229-228-8

J. Andrew Ross
SAP NetWeaver BI Accelerator
2008, 260 pp.
978-1-59229-192-2

Kumar Srinivasan, Sridhar Srinivasan
SAP NetWeaver BI Integrated Planning for Finance
2007, 318 pp.
978-1-59229-129-8

Dirk Herzog
ABAP Development for SAP NetWeaver BI: User Exits and BAdIs
2009, 266 pp.
978-1-59229-255-4

Peter Scott

SAP® BEx tools

Galileo Press

Bonn • Boston

ISBN 978-1-59229-279-0

© 2009 by Galileo Press Inc., Boston (MA)
2nd Edition updated 2009

Galileo Press is named after the Italian physicist, mathematician and philosopher Galileo Galilei (1564–1642). He is known as one of the founders of modern science and an advocate of our contemporary, heliocentric worldview. His words *Eppur si muove* (And yet it moves) have become legendary. The Galileo Press logo depicts Jupiter orbited by the four Galilean moons, which were discovered by Galileo in 1610.

Editor Erik Herman
Copy Editor Mike Beady
Cover Design Jill Winitzer
Photo Credit Image Copyright Susan McKenzie, 2008. Used under license from Shutterstock.com.
Layout Design Vera Brauner
Production Editor Kelly O'Callaghan
Typesetting Publishers' Design and Production Services, Inc.
Printed and bound in Canada

Contents

Acknowledgments

"We keep moving forward, opening new doors, and doing new things, because we're curious and curiosity keeps leading us down new paths." – Walt Disney.

First of all I'd like to thank the thousands of you who have read earlier editions of my SAP BEx Tools books and engaged us in consulting projects. I have learned as much from my colleagues and clients as I have taught in recent years.

The inspiration for this project comes from my continued passion to help organizations make better decisions. The waterfall impacts of making better decisions are enormous and include: improved efficiency, better profitability, higher compensation, and increased corporate social responsibility for all those who are impacted from that one initial decision. The ability to synthesize knowledge from data should become a priority with leading organizations looking for ways to establish and maintain a competitive advantage. In today's business climate, it is not cash, but knowledge which is king.

I expect you will find this book informative and easy to read. I am hopeful that it will provide you with some suggestions for overall deployment strategy while illustrating practical examples on how to stretch the value out of your SAP Business Intelligence platform.

Last but certainly not least, thank you to my friends at Galileo Press — for their guidance, patience, and support throughout the development of this book.

Happy Reading,
Peter

Introduction

The collection of reporting tools available with SAP NetWeaver Business Intelligence (BI) 7.0 is referred to as the Enterprise Reporting, Query, and Analysis Information Technology (IT) scenario. The core tools found in the BI suite are referred to as the Business Explorer (BEx). These BEx tools provide business users with the ability to design, create, analyze, and distribute data that results in improved decision-making capabilities.

The BEx suite is illustrated in Figure 1. The BEx suite is closely integrated with the SAP NetWeaver Portal and the Visual Composer modeling tool. Learning how to use the tools found in the BEx suite gives users the ability to create a query, format a report, publish Web applications, and distribute information to other business users.

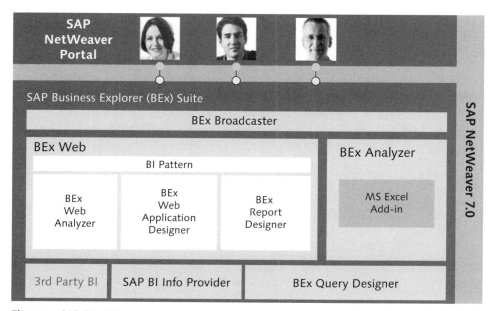

Figure 1 SAP BEx Suite

The BEx suite consists of the following tools:

- BEx Query Designer
- BEx Report Designer
- BEx Web Application Designer (WAD)
- BEx Web Analyzer (Web-based tool)
- BEx Analyzer (Excel-based tool)

Spanning across this toolset is the BEx Broadcaster, which provides options for scheduling and distributing report output to a printer, a Portable Document Format (PDF) file, or an email address. This book provides details on all of the BEx tools, including some advanced reporting features. It will also discuss the merger with Business Objects (BOBJ) and provide some direction on how to move forward as SAP BOBJ consolidates the BEx tools with the BOBJ portfolio.

The BEx Query Designer is the main tool for designing queries and generating data to analyze with an InfoProvider (i.e., InfoCube). The Query Designer lets a business user take advantage of Online Analytical Processing (OLAP) features such as variables, hierarchies, and custom formulas called calculated key figures. Defining exceptions or conditions and creating a customized matrix of rows and columns for a report is easily accomplished without any programming required. The Query Design tool is shown in Figure 2.

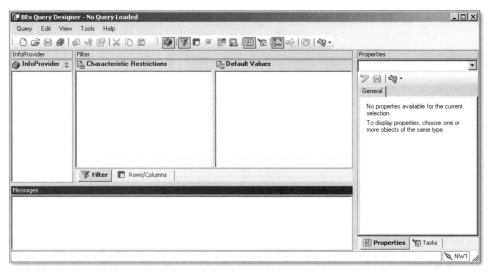

Figure 2 BEx Query Designer tool

The BEx Report Designer tool is a new as of BI 7.0. It has been added to the suite to fill the gap around formatted reporting. Earlier criticisms of SAP BW usually highlighted its inability to create presentation-quality reports. The Report Designer serves this purpose by taking the output from the Query Designer — a query definition — and transforming it by changing fonts, text, row/column heights, colors, etc. It also allows a designer to insert text, graphics, charts, headers, and footers. The result is a formatted report that is highly optimized for printing or for using in a presentation. A screenshot of the BEx Report Designer is shown in Figure 3.

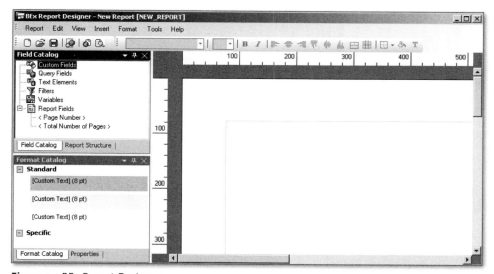

Figure 3 BEx Report Designer

The BEx WAD is another standalone tool that a report designer can use to build reporting applications that are optimized for the Web. A what-you-see-is-what-you-get (WYSIWYG) interface allows for the integration of basic word processing capabilities with BI-specific content. Web items delivered by SAP include buttons, filters, dropdown boxes, analysis grids, charts, and maps. All of these Web items represent placeholders that get assigned to a DataProvider. It is typically used by SAP power users to create interactive applications that are intuitive for end users to work with. Highly advanced dashboards can be constructed. If required, the underlying HTML code can also be modified or enhanced. The BEx WAD is depicted in Figure 4.

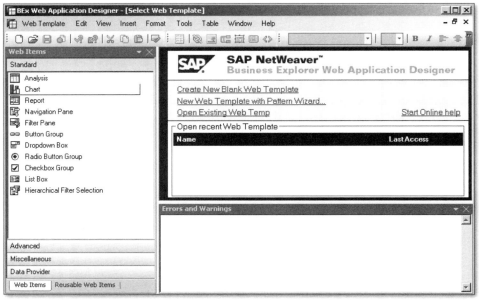

Figure 4   BEx WAD

The BEx Web Analyzer is an ad hoc analysis tool that is browser-based and provides zero footprints in terms of desktop application software because it requires no specific installation to use. The browser is linked to a specific SAP BI system and allows a user to drill down on a navigational state of a report and save this preferred view of the data for future use. OLAP functions, charting, broadcasting, exporting (to Excel or as a .csv file), and printing capabilities are all standard. A typical query executed in the BEx Web Analyzer is shown in Figure 5.

Figure 5   BEx Web Analyzer

The BEx Analyzer is integrated with Microsoft Excel and is accessible by installing the SAP Graphical User Interface (GUI) add-on for BI. Data is embedded into Microsoft Excel workbooks providing users with drag-and-drop capabilities to drill down and filter the data using SAP BI OLAP functions. Excel functions and features can be used to augment the analysis or to provide additional capabilities. Users can also leverage Visual Basic Applications (VBA) to create customized programs. As of BI 7.0, the BEx Analyzer comes with a second SAP BI–delivered toolbar that provides a rich set of design tools that allow for interactive applications to be constructed in a manner similar to that found in the SAP WAD. By using the new design mode a user can configure items such as dropdown boxes, checkboxes, and planning functions. Figure 6 is an illustration of a BEx workbook embedded in the BEx Analyzer.

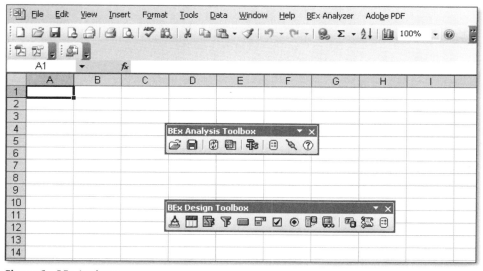

Figure 6   BEx Analyzer

The tools that make up the BEx suite provide solutions for enterprise reporting, ad hoc OLAP analysis, and dashboarding. The following chapters describe the BEx suite in detail and allow business users to stretch the value of their investment in SAP BI. Becoming an expert in BI Reporting can be achieved faster if you allow yourself to test the limitations of each tool. Experiment with each tool and try out every option. At the end of the day the worst thing a report designer can do is create a less than ideal report that can be cleaned up and enhanced over time. Be curious!

1 Fundamentals of Business Intelligence (BI) Reporting

It was once nearly impossible to extract information from applications. Corporate systems were disconnected, little historical information could be stored, and any data that was stored was often inaccessible. In addition, the information that was available lacked business process support. It is one thing to review data and quite another to link data to business processes that allow for exception reporting and alert notifications. These difficulties led to the concept of a *Data Warehouse* (DW).

1.1 Basics of Data Warehousing

Put simply, a DW serves as a decision support environment where corporate data can be quickly summarized at different operational levels.

Data warehousing is the process of choosing, migrating, cleaning, transforming, and storing data from disparate systems into one common location, whereby users can easily extract and analyze information for management decisions.

A DW is also commonly referred to as a:

▶ Data Mart

▶ Corporate Information Factory (CIF)

▶ Decision Support System (DSS)

▶ Business Intelligence (BI)

▶ Business Warehouse (BW)

One of the largest sources of data is an Enterprise Resource Planning (ERP) system. The process of migrating data from an ERP system to a DW is usually referred to as *Extraction, Transformation, and Loading* (ETL).

The multidimensional analysis offered by a DW, which enables DW users to analyze data trends, exceptions, and variances of interest, is called *Online Analytical Processing* (OLAP). Typical OLAP is used to answer questions such as:

- ▸ What was my best-selling product in January?
- ▸ What are my year-to-date Cost Center expenses?
- ▸ Why was I under my revenue target for March?
- ▸ Are we gaining or losing market share this month?
- ▸ How will my year-end look?

To compete, companies need to disseminate knowledge and information throughout their organization. To do that they have to contend with massive amounts of data that arrive from many different sources at various times. The ultimate goal of data warehousing is to manage this complexity and provide users with knowledge that gives them a competitive advantage and operational excellence.

The results of a successful data-warehousing initiative should include faster decision times, improved information quality, and greater strategic insight. With data warehousing, the data itself becomes a key asset to an organization, but only if decision makers can successfully access, understand, and leverage this new knowledge effectively.

Anyone in an organization that makes decisions needs BI; in other words, everybody. BI supports decisions at every level within an organization, whether the information is for an executive officer looking at Key Performance Indicators (KPIs) or for a finance manager to rationalize and monitor expenses by cost elements. The strategic nature of an executive dashboard and the tactical nature of a cost center analysis require data with the right level of detail and in the right context.

The concept of today's DW evolved from the concept of Management Information Systems (MIS) from IBM in the '60s and from a Harvard Business School article on Executive Information Systems (EIS) in the '70s. Data warehousing became prominent following the research and publications of Bill Inmon and Ralph Kimball. In 1958, Hans Peter Luhn defined BI systems in the *IBM Journal*. In the early 1990s, a Gartner analyst, Howard Dresner, popularized the term BI as a general term that describes using facts to improve decision making. Since then, BI and data warehousing have become a top spending priority for organizations and Chief Information Officers.

With numerous vendors in the data-warehousing space, BI tools have become standardized into familiar categories that are designed to report, analyze, and present data. These tools are generally categorized as:

- ▶ Spreadsheets
- ▶ Reporting and Querying
- ▶ OLAP
- ▶ Web Applications
- ▶ Dashboards
- ▶ Business Process Management (BPM)
- ▶ Data Mining

1.2 Basics of SAP BI

SAP BI is an end-to-end data-warehousing solution that is usually built on a three-tier environment consisting of Development (DEV), Test (Quality Assurance (QA)), and Production (PROD) servers. This three-tier configuration separates development work from a live system, and allows for sufficient testing with real data in the QA system. Enhancements are transported through a well-defined process that moves from DEV to QA for testing, and then to PROD, where BI users can access information. This landscape is depicted in Figure 1.1.

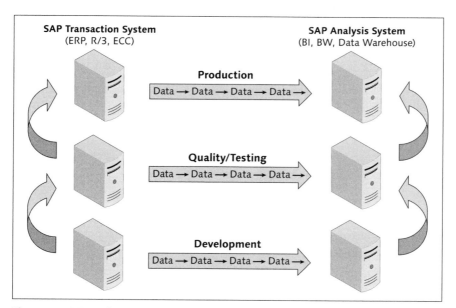

Figure 1.1 A Typical SAP ERP and SAP BI Landscape

SAP BI also has a three-tiered architecture. Figure 1.2 summarizes the architecture, which consists of the following layers:

▶ **Presentation layer**
Consists of the SAP Business Explorer (BEx) tools such as BEx Analyzer and BEx Web Application Designer (WAD).

▶ **Database layer**
Consists of InfoCubes, Data Store Objects (DSO), MultiCubes, and Master Data Objects that can be reported on. This layer also includes the Administrator Workbench and ETL capabilities.

▶ **Source Systems layer**
Consists of SAP ERP Central Component (ECC) or ERP systems, legacy systems, text files, or another SAP BI environment that serves at a Data Mart.

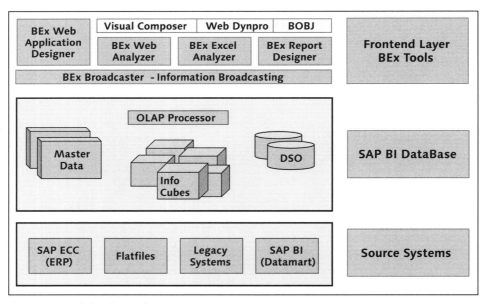

Figure 1.2 High-level BI Architecture

All SAP BI queries are constructed using the BEx tools, which request data from the BI database. The BI database follows an ETL process to populate InfoCubes, DSO, MultiCubes, and Master Data.

Objects for which queries can be created against or executed on using BEx tools are collectively referred to as *InfoProviders*. An *InfoCube*, which is a type of InfoProvider, is a subset or collection of data from the BI database that has logical relationships that allow users to report on many things simultaneously. The InfoCube is based on SAP's extended star schema model.

Queries are designed and developed with the *BEx Query Designer*. A completed query is referred to as a *Data Provider*. You can display the output of a query definition as either a Web report using a standard web browser, such as Microsoft's Internet Explorer 7, or view a query result using the BEx Analyzer, which is integrated with Microsoft Excel.

Many queries can be built from a single InfoProvider. A single query definition has a one-to-one relationship with its InfoProvider. The query results from a query definition are displayed on a web page, or in the BEx Analyzer. You can format and store query results with many different views, which can result in a many-to-one relationship between a query definition and the formatted query results. Figure 1.3 displays these relationships.

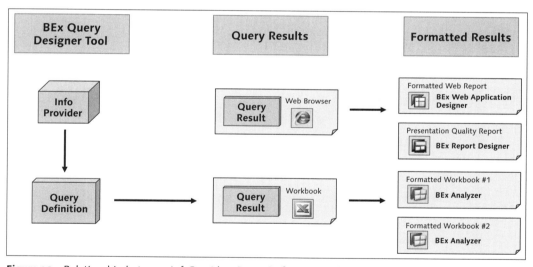

Figure 1.3 Relationship between InfoProvider, Query Definition, and Formatted Results

1.3 BEx Tools

The analytics architecture of SAP NetWeaver BI provides functionality for reporting, analysis, and planning of all business data. In general, the following scenarios are possible:

▶ A complete data-warehousing toolset that allows simple access, integration, and analysis of relational and analytical data from SAP and non-SAP data sources.

▶ The integration of analytical and planning capabilities into operational processes.

▶ A multienvironment platform that enables drill-down navigation and slice-and-dice analysis of data.

▶ The ability to distribute reports to information requesters.

SAP BEx reporting tools allow users to create, locate, execute, view, format, manage, schedule, and precalculate reports. Many of the BEx tools in SAP BI are installed on a client workstation using the SAP GUI and installing the BI add-on.

The primary BEx tools, shown in Figure 1.4, included with SAP NetWeaver 7.0 BI are:

▶ BEx Analyzer

▶ BEx Query Designer

▶ BEx Web Analyzer

▶ BEx WAD

▶ BEx Report Designer

▶ BEx Broadcaster and Information Broadcasting

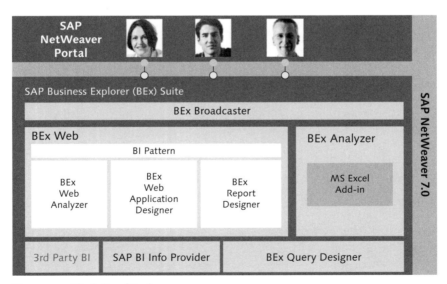

Figure 1.4 BEx Suite of Tools

Most organizations define user communities that result in certain tool access being assigned to each user community. At a minimum, this definition typically involves end users and power users. Depending on the particular scenario within an organization, the vast majority of end users will not have access to the design tools and will simply execute workbooks using the BEx Analyzer or view reports on a web page. The design tools would then be assigned only to power users. Design tools are the BEx Query Designer, BEx WAD, and the BEx Report Designer. By using SAP authorization concepts an administrator can assign standard security objects, which allow for the establishment of a predefined power user role and an end user role to limit access to tools based on the responsibilities of each user community. A proposal on how to split the roles and responsibilities between end users and power users can be found in Figure 1.5.

Role:	BI Power User	BI End User
Primary Responsibilities:	• Understand the underlying data in the SAP ERP system and the data in the BI system • Able to reconcile data across ERP and BI systems • Ability to create Ad-hoc queries • Provide first Level Support to End Users including report navigation training • Make recommendations for changes/enhancements to queries and reports to IT • Distribute reports to End Users • Consults with IT when in need of assistance	• A report consumer • Ability to log in to the SAP BI system and successfully execute a desired report • Ability to interpret report results and make business decisions using the data • Distributes BI reports to non-SAP users • Consults with power users when in need of assistance
BI Tools Used:	• BEx Query Designer • BEx Analyzer and/or BEx Web Reporting • BEx Broadcaster	• BEx Analyzer and/or BEx Web Reporting

Figure 1.5 Definition of Power Users versus End Users

In addition to the standard BEx BI tools, the BEx Browser is a tool that was part of the BW 3.x toolset. This tool is no longer available with the SAP NetWeaver 7.0 BI tools; however, it is part of the SAP BI add-on installation that, by default, will install the BW 3.x tools along with the newer BI 7.0 tools.

The *BEx Browser* is a graphical desktop-like tool used to launch queries and workbooks and categorize them into roles, favorites, and folders. The BEx Browser also incorporates standard shortcut functionality, which enables you to access documents, Windows applications, Internet URLs, and SAP R/3 transactions from a single interface. The BEx Browser allows users to create folders to organize their content. Figure 1.6 illustrates how BI content can be linked with other business tools in the BEx Browser.

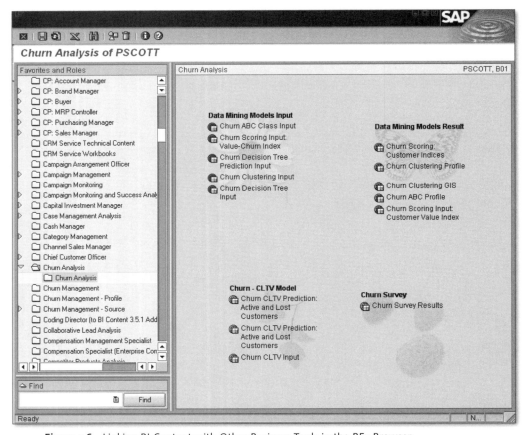

Figure 1.6 Linking BI Content with Other Business Tools in the BEx Browser

The BEx Browser toolbar (shown in Figure 1.7) contains the following icons:

▶ Exit

▶ Save

▶ Refresh

▶ Start Business Explorer Analyzer

- ▶ Find
- ▶ New Folder
- ▶ Delete
- ▶ About SAP BI Browser
- ▶ Help

Figure 1.7 BEx Browser Toolbar

You create content within the BEx Browser on the right side of the screen. Right-clicking on a blank part of the screen displays a context menu with several options. You can create the following links within a folder (Figure 1.8 displays the available options):

- ▶ Folder
- ▶ Workbook
- ▶ Internet Address (URL)
- ▶ SAP Transaction
- ▶ Document (Word, PowerPoint)
- ▶ Shortcut (to other applications on a local PC)

Figure 1.8 Adding New Content to a Folder

Each folder created for a role or user favorites can be further customized by assigning a background symbol and color, which are translucent. There are eight backgrounds and colors to choose from, each of which has a nature theme.

To customize folder options, right-click on a folder on the right side of the BEx Browser window and select Choose symbol and color. The graphical options are displayed in Figure 1.9.

Figure 1.9 Folders Customized with Background Symbol and Color

The *BEx Analyzer* is the primary reporting environment for SAP BI. Most users find it very intuitive because it is integrated with Microsoft Excel. You can add Excel calculations, notes, charts, and graphics to a single worksheet and insert multiple reports into a workbook, thereby creating a package of reports. The BEx Analyzer combines the power of OLAP with all of Excel's functionality. You can also use *Visual Basic for Applications* (VBA).

As of BI 7.0 the BEx Analyzer is also a sophisticated design tool with planning input capabilities. The BEx Analyzer's functionality is divided into two different modes, each with its own toolbar (shown in Figure 1.10) and functions.

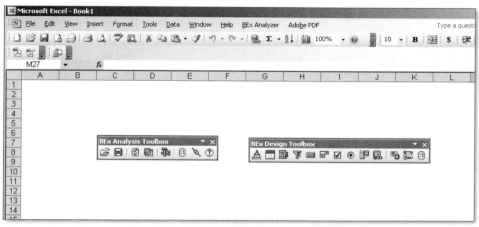

Figure 1.10 Analyzer Toolbars Found in SAP NetWeaver BI 7.0

The two modes are the Analysis mode and the Design mode. The BEx Analysis toolbar is used to perform OLAP analyses on query results in a workbook environment. Working in Analysis mode, you can navigate interactively on the data by filtering, drilling down, and sorting. Analysis mode also provides access to the planning functionality, the BEx Query Designer, and the BEx Broadcaster. A summary of the BEx Analysis toolbar is shown in Figure 1.11.

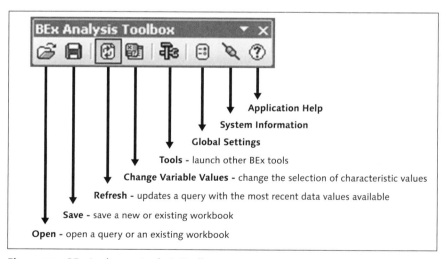

Figure 1.11 BEx Analyzer—Analysis Toolbar

The BEx Design toolbar is used to create custom templates and interfaces for query applications within the workbook. Working in design mode allows a user to insert BI design items, such as analysis grids, dropdown boxes, radio button groups, checkboxes, and a filter blocks. Microsoft Excel functionality can also be used to insert titles, images, formulas, and text to enrich the presentation of the template. Figure 1.12 highlights the available design items. Design mode is toggled on and off using the BEx Design toolbar.

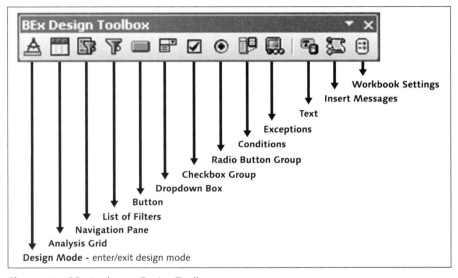

Figure 1.12   BEx Analyzer—Design Toolbar

By default, the BEx Analyzer provides a standard design template that is leveraged every time query results are embedded into a workbook. This default template consists of an analysis grid, filter block, information button, and a chart button that toggles the data between a graphical representation and a table view. The default template, which appears in Figure 1.13, also displays the author of the query, by user ID, and displays the status of the data—which is the date and time of the last ETL process that brought data records into the InfoProvider, which feeds the query results.

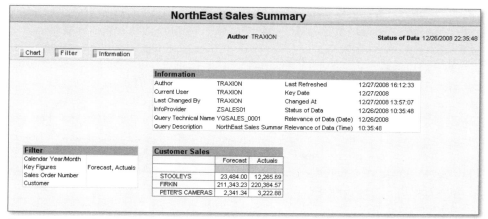

Figure 1.13 Standard Layout for a BEx Analyzer Workbook

The *BEx Query Designer* is a standalone application that enables users to build complex query definitions without using programming. All subsequent BI reporting and analysis is based on query definitions. The BEx Query Designer is displayed in Figure 1.14.

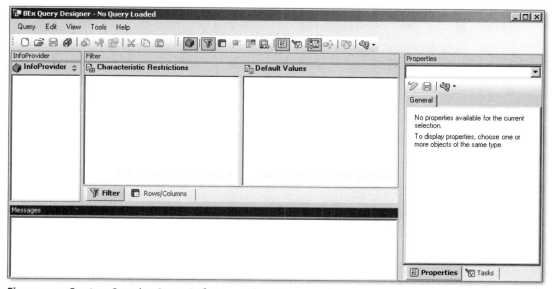

Figure 1.14 Create a Complex Query Definition without Programming

The BEx Query Designer can be launched from the BEx folder—typically found under the Start menu of a Windows-based system. It may also be accessed from the BEx Analyzer or the BEx WAD. A query definition that is created and saved using the Query Designer can be viewed using the BEx Analyzer or it can be viewed using the *BEx Web Analyzer*—also referred to as Web reporting. The BEx Web Analyzer provides a standalone Web application for data analysis that is called by entering or copying a Web address or URL into a browser. In addition, the Web Analyzer can be used to save data views generated from the navigation and analysis of a standard query layout. These query views allow users to return to a preferred navigational state in the future and view results using this view. OLAP functionality is available in both the BEx Analyzer and Web report. The BEx Analyzer requires software installation on a user's PC while the Web report has the advantage of being "zero footprint"—it requires no additional software except a standard web browser. The standard Web-reporting interface is shown in Figure 1.15.

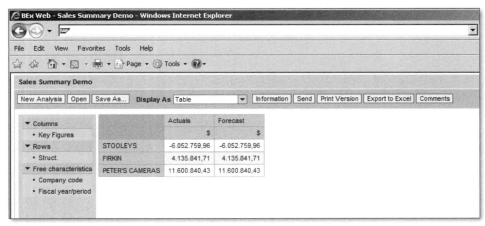

Figure 1.15   Standard Layout for a Web Report

The *BEx WAD* is a desktop application that is very similar to other web page authoring tools. The BEx WAD, Microsoft FrontPage, and Adobe Dreamweaver are alike in that they all enable you to use a what-you-see-is-what-you-get (WYSIWYG) environment when creating a web page. One unique feature of the WAD, depicted in Figure 1.16, is that it enables a designer to incorporate BI data and predefined BI objects, along with standard HTML code and Web design application programming interfaces (APIs). These BI-specific objects retrieve BI data from an SAP BI data provider and place it on the web page. These objects are referred to as Web items. Some of the available Web items included with the WAD are:

- ▸ Charts
- ▸ Navigation Pane
- ▸ Filter Pane
- ▸ Dropdown Box
- ▸ Checkbox Group
- ▸ Tab Pages
- ▸ Maps
- ▸ Menu Bar
- ▸ Information Fields
- ▸ List of Exceptions
- ▸ List of Conditions
- ▸ Ticker

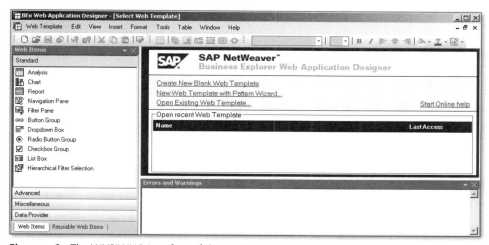

Figure 1.16 The WYSIWYG Interface of the WAD

The *BEx Report Designer is a* graphical tool for creating highly formatted static reports typically optimized for presentation or printing. It is a standalone desktop application that is launched from the BEx folder. The formatted report can be displayed on the Web or converted into a PDF document to be printed or distributed. It is typically used for common financial statements such as balance sheets and income statements. Note: To create a formatted report there must be a structure used in the Columns section of the query for which the report is sourced from.

The Report Designer, shown in Figure 1.17, is a new tool that shipped with SAP NetWeaver BI 7.0 and has some basic functionality that quickly allows a designer to build a report optimized for presentation.

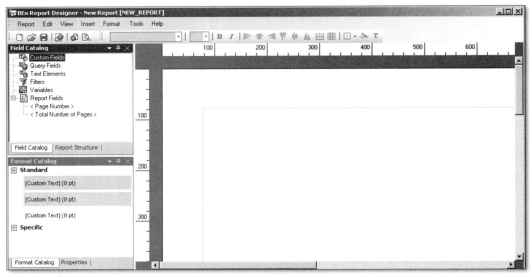

Figure 1.17 The BEx Report Designer Tool

Some of the BEx Report Designer functions include:

► Inserting rows and columns

► Adjusting the height and width of rows and columns

► Dragging and dropping the position of individual fields

► Adding text and text headings

► Inserting report or page headers and footers

► Basic formatting functions such as font, font size, font enhancements (bold, italic, etc.), font colors, and background colors

► Inserting pictures, images, and charts

► Formatting row, cell, and column borders

► Merging cells

The *BEx Broadcaster* is used to precalculate and distribute reports, queries, Web templates, query views, and workbooks. The precalculated results can be prepared as a document or as a Web URL that can be accessed as a link. The advantage here is that precalculating shortens the wait time for users and reduces the workload on the servers during peak hours. The distribution options allow broadcasting to email(s), portals, or precalculated reports to be sent to a printer. With NetWeaver BI 7.0 the broadcasting capabilities are typically configured using the Broadcasting Wizard. The Wizard provides an assisted set of predefined steps that support a user creating a new broadcast setting. It is possible to broadcast by email or to a Portal at a recurring time/date specified by the user or by a trigger, such as when data is updated in the Info-Provider. Certain authorizations are required to create and schedule background jobs. This access is usually only given to a limited number of users, who can then configure broadcast settings that propagate to a department or set of information consumers.

The BEx Broadcaster can be launched from many of the other primary BEx publishing tools. Regardless of the launch point, the same series of steps are followed to create a new broadcast setting.

You can call the BEx Broadcaster using the toolbars from the:

▶ BEx Query Designer: QUERY • PUBLISH • BEx BROADCASTER

▶ BEx Analyzer Analysis toolbar: TOOLS • BROADCASTER

▶ BEx Report Designer: REPORT • PUBLISH • BEx BROADCASTER

▶ BEx WAD • PUBLISH • BEx BROADCASTER

Tip
The Broadcast option only appears in the BEx Analyzer when a workbook has been opened. It is also possible to launch the BEx Broadcaster from a Web report by right-clicking on the context menu over the results area and following the Broadcast and Export menu.

The overall workflow for using all of the various BEx tools is shown in Figure 1.18. The most basic reporting is accomplished by using the BEx Query Designer and the BEx Analyzer. An alternative or complementary reporting strategy to just using the BEx Analyzer is to use Web-based reporting. With Web reporting, you don't have to install any software on a user's PC, which is why this alternative is known as a zero-footprint solution. Query designers can publish formatted, graphical reports using the BEx WAD and distribute these reports via URLs or a preexisting intranet portal. High-end formatting can be achieved by leveraging the Reporting Agent, Download Scheduler, or via integration with Crystal Reports.

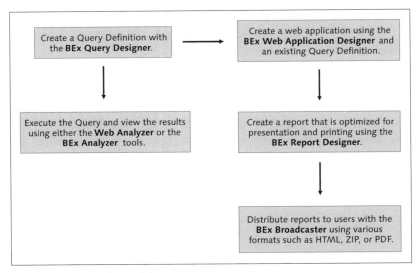

Figure 1.18   BEx Tools Workflow

1.4   Summary

SAP BI has evolved into a full-fledged DW. The suite of BEx tools allow users with diverse backgrounds to effectively access and analyze data in a timely fashion. Queries are defined using the BEx Query Designer and analyzed within the BEx Analyzer or within a BEx Web Application. Additional formatting can be achieved with the BEx Report Designer or by leveraging the new Design toolbar found in the BEx Analyzer. Highly interactive dashboards and Web applications can be developed using the BEx WAD. Charting and graphics features in the WAD allow for quick processing of complex sets of data. The BEx Broadcaster offers the ability to distribute a variety of objects with BI content to a spectrum of users according to individual requirements. Each BEx tool has a primary function and deliverable that is then integrated with and passed along to other BEx tools for further development. This book focuses on the step-by-step processes of creating a query, viewing results, formatting reports, and coordinating the distribution of knowledge and information. The next chapter will look at the BEx Query Designer in detail.

2 The Business Explorer (BEx) Query Designer

The BEx Query Designer is a standalone application accessed from the Windows Start menu.

2.1 Overview of the BEx Query Designer

To access the BEx Query Designer, follow the menu path: START • PROGRAMS • BUSINESS EXPLORER • QUERY DESIGNER (see Figure 2.1).

Note

The specific menu path may differ, depending on the installation version of the SAP GUI software. When installing the SAP GUI the Business Intelligence (BI) add-on must be included to install the BEx tools on a client's machine.

Figure 2.1   Navigating to the BEx Query Designer

Launching the Query Designer prompts you to log on to a specific SAP BI system (see Figure 2.2).

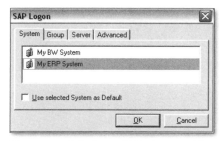

Figure 2.2   Selecting a BI Environment from the SAP Logon Pad

From the SAP Logon pad in the System tab, select the appropriate BI environment, and click OK.

The BI system then prompts you for valid logon credentials (see Figure 2.3). Enter the following information:

► Client (#)

► User (ID)

► Password

► Language (two-digit code. "EN"—English, "FR"—French)

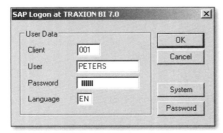

Figure 2.3 Logging On to SAP BI

The initial view of the BEx Query Designer is shown in Figure 2.4.

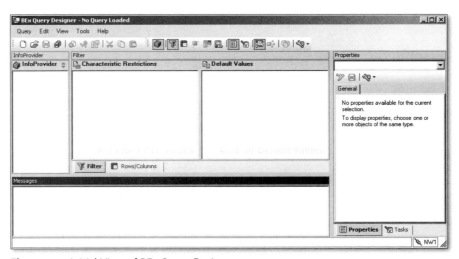

Figure 2.4 Initial View of BEx Query Designer

2.2   Query Designer Layout

The Query Designer is a graphical standalone application that allows InfoProviders to access datasets. Some examples of InfoProviders are:

► Data Store Objects (DSO)

► InfoCubes

► Master Data

► InfoSets

► MultiProviders (MultiCubes)

Query definitions are created from InfoProviders. No programming knowledge is required to create a query. Users can simply drag and drop specific elements from an InfoProvider and build an entire query definition using the BEx Query Designer toolbar.

In addition to the toolbar, the BEx Query Designer is made up of five key sections. The left-most section of the Query Designer, which displays all data available for a particular InfoProvider, is considered to be the *source* pane. The four remaining panes are *destination* panes, which are used to create and format a query definition. The following sections constitute the destination panes:

► Filter

► Rows/Columns

► Properties

► Messages

Selecting and combining InfoObjects from the InfoProvider and placing them in specific destination panes determines the default layout of a report. InfoObjects can be either characteristics or key figures. To create a simple query, users arrange characteristics and key figures in the rows or columns to establish an initial view for the query analysis.

Table 2.1 lists the BEx Query Designer panes and describes each of their respective behaviors.

BEx Query Designer Panes	Behavior
InfoProvider pane	Provides a hierarchical listing of all structures, characteristics, variables, and key figures available from a particular InfoProvider (InfoCube, DSO, MultiCube). These elements are the building blocks for a new query definition.
Filter pane	Filters are applied to restrict data to certain values. You can restrict a query to a certain Company Code or to certain time periods. For example, placing Calendar Year in the Filter pane and restricting the InfoObject to 2006.
	The filter pane has two elements to it. One is called Characteristic restrictions and the other Default values. There is a subtle difference between these two elements. Defining a restriction under Default values sets an initial filter status when a query is executed. This filter can be removed or adjusted by a user during navigation.
	Defining a restriction under Characteristic restrictions will hard code the filter so that the setting cannot be removed during navigation by a user.
	For example, if a fiscal year value of 2009 is placed into the Characteristic restrictions area of the Filter pane, then a user will not be able to fetch data for any other fiscal year.
	If a fiscal year value of 2009 is placed into the Default values area of the Filter pane, then a user can remove this filter during query navigation and pick another year(s) to analyze in the InfoProvider.
Rows/Columns pane	The Rows/Columns pane consists of four elements:
	Rows
	InfoObjects placed in Rows are added to a report and displayed by default. Characteristics and key figures can be combined in this pane.
	Columns
	InfoObjects placed in Columns are added to a report and displayed by default. Characteristics and key figures can be combined in this pane.

Table 2.1 Summary of BEx Query Designer Panes

BEx Query Designer Panes	Behavior
	Free Characteristics
	InfoObjects placed in Free Characteristics are added to a report, but are not displayed in the report output unless requested by a user. This allows a query definition to be constructed with numerous fields that can be displayed, but only when requested by the user.
	Preview
	The Preview section provides a very basic representation of a report template. Only objects found in the Rows and Columns panes appear in the Preview pane.
Properties	The Properties pane provides a set of individual settings for each query component found in the query definition. The properties allow settings for Characteristics, Key Figures, Variables, Conditions, Exceptions, etc., to be defined and modified based on the overall requirements. The property dialog changes depending on which specific component is clicked on.
	One or more objects/components of the same type can be selected and modified at the same time. For example, select multiple key figures by defining the number of decimal places as 0.00 using the Properties pane dialog for Key Figures.
Messages	The Messages pane supplies system messages, warnings, and other information depending on the state of the current query definition. From the context menu of the message, you can navigate to the actual error or display information about the error.

Table 2.1 Summary of BEx Query Designer Panes (Cont.)

In summary, placing objects from an InfoProvider into various destination panes builds a default view of a report (anything in the Rows and Columns panes), and allows for additional information to be presented if it is selected during report navigation (Free Characteristics). Users can navigate to a query definition to build their own version of a report by deciding what objects they would like to see and in what order they want the objects to appear. Users can specify the order by shuffling InfoObjects found in the Rows, Columns, and Free Characteristics panes. Any characteristics placed only in the Filter pane are not available for users to display in their report output.

For example, a query definition is constructed with the following objects in each pane:

- ▶ Free Characteristics pane
  - ▶ Sales Order (Characteristic)
  - ▶ Calendar Year/Month (Characteristic)
- ▶ Rows pane
  - ▶ Controlling Area (Characteristic)
  - ▶ Company Code (Characteristic)
  - ▶ Customer (Characteristic)
- ▶ Columns pane
  - ▶ Revenue (Key Figure)
  - ▶ Costs (Key Figure)
  - ▶ Profit (Calculated Key Figure)
  - ▶ Margin % (Calculated Key Figure)

The query definition for this example is displayed within the BEx Query Designer tool (see Figure 2.5 for the layout). The default layout for the report displays what is in the Rows and Columns panes. The additional objects found in the Free Characteristics pane provide additional detail and analysis if a user chooses to drill down on those characteristics. The default layout and results for this sample query definition are shown in Figure 2.6.

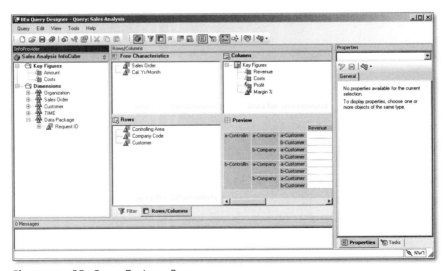

Figure 2.5   BEx Query Designer Panes

The flexibility of a query definition is determined by the contents of the Free Characteristics pane. By default, the report only displays the Controlling Area, Company Code, Customer, and four key figures. The individual orders for each customer are not displayed in the default view; however, a user can easily display this information with a click of the mouse. Another user may require the calendar month for each order to be listed in the output. Therefore, many users can employ the same basic report by simply leveraging the information in the Free Characteristics pane.

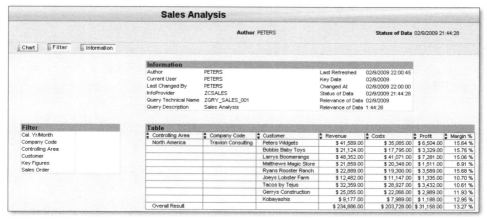

Figure 2.6 A Simple Sales Analysis Query Definition

2.3   Using the BEx Query Designer Toolbar

The BEx Query Designer toolbar consists of the following icons:

- ▸ New Query
- ▸ Open Query
- ▸ Save Query
- ▸ Save All
- ▸ Execute
- ▸ Check Query
- ▸ Query Properties
- ▸ Cut/Copy/Paste
- ▸ InfoProvider
- ▸ Filter

- ▸ Rows/Columns
- ▸ Cell Definitions
- ▸ Conditions
- ▸ Exceptions
- ▸ Properties
- ▸ Tasks
- ▸ Messages
- ▸ Documents
- ▸ Technical Names

Each of these icons is discussed throughout this chapter. Depending on the current state of a query definition, certain icons and functionality may not be available. When a specific icon or tool is not available, the icon will be grayed-out. The Query Designer toolbar is displayed in Figure 2.7.

Figure 2.7 Query Design Toolbar

2.4 Accessing InfoProviders

Launching the BEx Query Designer and logging on to the preferred SAP BI environment is the first step in creating a query definition. The next step requires a user to pick a functional area of the BI database, usually designated by an Info-Cube, which contains information of interest (see Figure 2.8).

MultiCubes and InfoCubes are the preferred InfoProviders to report on. They offer better performance than DSO, and contain multiple dimensions that make them more useful to business analysts when building reports.

To access and view the information in an InfoProvider, click on the New Query icon in the BEx Query Designer toolbar. A pop-up window opens and displays all of the available InfoProviders. Depending on standard SAP roles and security profiles, each user may see only a subset of all of the available InfoCubes, DSO objects, and MultiCubes. InfoProviders are grouped by InfoAreas, which are simply folders that group InfoProviders with similar functional data.

Navigate through the folder structure until you locate the InfoProvider you want. Double-click on an individual InfoCube or MultiCube to bring it into the Query Designer.

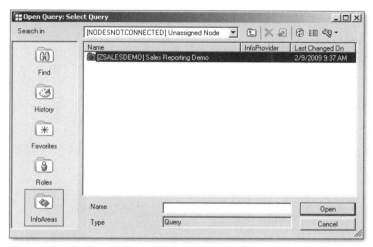

Figure 2.8 Finding Available InfoProviders in InfoAreas

Note

If the description or technical name of an InfoProvider is well known, you can use this text as a search string to navigate through the InfoArea hierarchy quickly. To search for a specific cube, click on the Find icon (pair of binoculars) located in the toolbar of the Select InfoProvider window (see Figure 2.9). In this example, we searched for an InfoCube with the keyword "sales" found in the description.

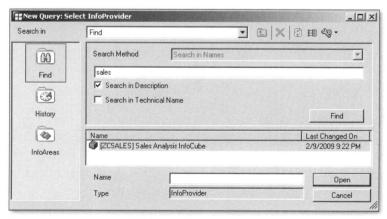

Figure 2.9 Search for InfoCubes

Once loaded into the Query Designer, an InfoProvider appears in the left-most pane of the screen (see Figure 2.10). It is structured into three folders:

▶ Key Figures

▶ Dimensions

▶ Structures

You may only see a Key Figure folder and a Dimensions folder. Structures are usually created by power users to resave complex work done in either a row or column structure. These structures are described in more detail later.

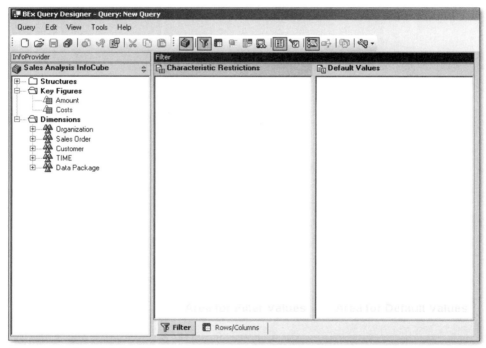

Figure 2.10 Open InfoProvider Displayed in Left Pane of Query Designer

Some examples of *key figures* are quantities, amounts, and values. *Dimensions* are groupings of characteristics that logically fit together. A dimension labeled "Customer" will usually include characteristics such as Customer Number, Sold-to Party, Address, and Country. *Characteristics* are qualitative fields that describe key figures. Cost Center and Sales Region are also examples of characteristics.

Structures are created by query designers after an InfoProvider has been made available. Because structures are reusable, work that has been completed in one query can be used in other queries. A combination of characteristics and key figures, in a particular order, with specific filters, can be saved back to the InfoProvider as a structure.

When future queries are developed from the same InfoProvider, this reusable structure can be added to a new query via drag and drop. This allows for the rapid development of queries that use common sets of columns or rows. It also facilitates the easy maintenance of multiple queries; for example, adjusting the structure members for a single query will immediately update all queries that use the same row or column structure.

Updating all of the queries using a common structure is not always wanted or recommended. Often, it can be helpful to use an existing structure to expedite query development and then to sever all ties to the global structure. Removing the global reference of this structure (that is tied to an InfoProvider) protects a query from unwanted changes in the future when the structure is changed. Essentially, this allows a query designer to reuse objects and then break the reference to the original object, allowing for different versions to exist. To remove the global reference, right-click on a structure in a query definition (see Figure 2.11) and select Remove Reference.

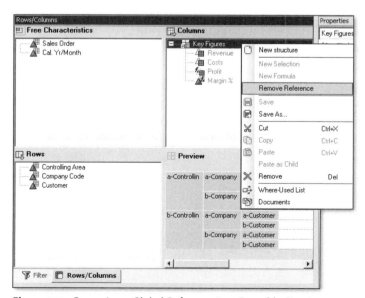

Figure 2.11 Removing a Global Reference to a Reusable Structure

To add a structure, key figure, or characteristic to a query definition, simply drag and drop the item from the InfoProvider source pane to the appropriate destination pane. To remove an item from a query definition, highlight the selected item and press Delete or drag and drop the item back to the InfoProvider source pane. Figure 2.12 shows the beginnings of a query definition.

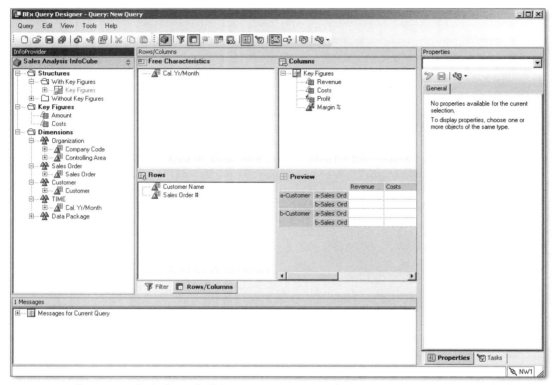

Figure 2.12 Basic Query Definition

Technically, it is possible to include up to 50 characteristics in the rows and the columns. Every structure found in the query definition decreases this total of 50 by 1. A query definition can have, at most, two structures, so for all practical purposes a limit of 48 characteristics is more appropriate.

Efficient query design comes from a solid understanding of both the BI functionality available in the Query Designer and also from having the background business knowledge about the underlying data that is available to report against. Trying to design reports without both these components is difficult. Understanding all of the available Online Analytical Processing (OLAP) functions allows a designer to take advantage of the inherent flexibility in the Query Designer while quickly arranging the output.

2.5 Creating a Basic Query Definition

The following steps outline a methodology for developing a query and take into account the underlying functionality and efficiency considerations of the BEx Query Designer.

1. Click on the New Query icon in the BEx Query Designer toolbar.
2. Locate and select the desired InfoProvider.
3. Drag and drop preexisting structures to the Rows pane or Columns pane. Remove the global reference for these reusable objects, if necessary.
4. Drag and drop characteristics to the Rows or Free Characteristics panes.
5. Restrict values for characteristics under the Default Values section in the Filter pane.
6. Format each characteristic found in the Rows and Free Characteristics panes by selecting each one and then using the Properties pane dialog.
7. Drag and drop key figures to the Columns pane.
8. Create any required Restricted Key Figures (RKFs).
9. Create any required Calculated Key Figures (CKFs).
10. Format each key figure found in the Columns pane by selecting each one (together or individually) and using the Properties pane dialog.
11. Add characteristic value variables for characteristics found in the Rows, Filter, and Free Characteristics panes.
12. Click on the Exception icon in the BEx Query Designer toolbar to define exceptions.
13. Click on the Condition icon in the BEx Query Designer toolbar to define conditions.
14. Click on the Query Properties icon in the BEx Query Designer toolbar to adjust the overall query properties.
15. Click on the Check Query icon in the BEx Query Designer toolbar to check the query syntax. Note: This checks for syntax errors—not logic errors.

16. Save the query with the Save Query icon in the BEx Query Designer toolbar.

17. Click on the Execute icon in the BEx Query Designer toolbar to execute and test the query in a web browser.

18. Select QUERY • PUBLISH in the BEx Query Designer menubar to publish the query to a role, portal, or BEx Broadcaster.

SAP BI categorizes existing query definitions and InfoProviders to assist with general navigation in the system. When you click on the New Query or Open Query icons in the BEx Query Designer toolbar, a pop-up window with the following categories appears:

▶ **History**
Displays recently accessed queries/InfoProviders

▶ **InfoAreas**
Lists all available InfoProviders organized into functional folders

▶ **Roles**
Lists all accessible public folders/queries

▶ **Favorites**
Lists all queries in a private folder specific to the user

2.6   Modifying InfoObject Properties

The BEx Query Designer toolbar has a wealth of functionality from which to choose. In this section, starting with a basic query definition, we'll explain how you can take advantage of many of the key features of this tool.

To create a new query definition, as seen in Figure 2.13, do the following:

1. Click on the New Query icon.

2. Choose an InfoProvider from the History or InfoArea tabs.

3. The contents of the InfoProvider will load into the InfoProvider pane of the BEx Query Designer.

4. Drag and drop characteristics and key figures into the new query definition. Place one or more key figure in the Columns pane, and one or more characteristics in each of the Rows, and Free Characteristics panes.

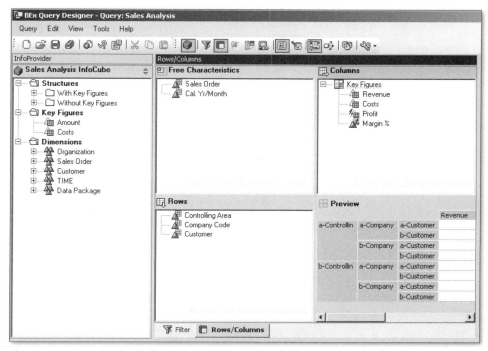

Figure 2.13 Example of a Basic Query Definition

By default, objects added to a query definition are formatted based on the configuration parameters for the InfoObject and key figures when they were created in the BI system. The descriptions of these objects may not be ideal for the report developer. Other display properties, such as showing totals, changing the positioning of negative numbers, and the number of decimal places, are all defined within the BEx Query Designer.

To access the Properties dialog for characteristics, simply highlight the intended object and use the Properties pane to make any necessary adjustments.

The Description field allows a query designer to replace the default Description of the InfoObject. This Description field is displayed as the column heading when a report is executed (see Figure 2.14). Later on the standard text for the characteristic can be restored by clicking the Use Standard Text box found just below the Description field.

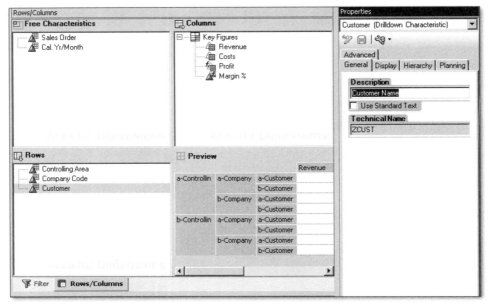

Figure 2.14   Basic Query Definition with a New Description Defined for a Characteristic

Under the Display tab of the Properties pane, the Display As drop-down box allows a characteristic to be displayed as a key, as text, or as a combination of both.

The Results Rows drop-down box allows a query definition to summarize results based on the individual values of the characteristic. Results rows can always be suppressed (not displayed), always displayed, or conditionally displayed if more than one unique result for a characteristic value is found. When creating new query definitions, it is recommended that you turn off results rows to avoid confusion. During runtime, they can always be added to a navigational state of a report by a user, if required.

Other options available from the Characteristic Properties menu include access to hierarchies and hierarchy properties. There is a shortcut to set common properties for all of the characteristics found in a query definition. Multiselect is possible by holding down the CTRL key and choosing multiple characteristics found in the rows. Once highlighted, these characteristics will all be affected by any changes made in the Properties pane. Some other properties related to characteristics can be seen in Figure 2.15.

Figure 2.15   Display Properties for Characteristics

Key figures have similar options that are also accessed through the Properties pane. Select a key figure located in the Columns pane of a Query Definition and look in the Properties pane for the available options.

You can replace the column heading by overwriting the text in the Description field. Turning on Highlighting will italicize the entire Key Figure column when the report is executed. Scaling factors allow you to reduce the number of values displayed in a report. A scaling factor of 1,000 will divide all values for the key figure by 1,000 and show the scaling factor in the execute report, just below the column description. You can also format the number of decimal places by choosing an appropriate setting from the Number of Decimal Places drop-down box. Some of the available options for key figure properties are shown in Figure 2.16.

Figure 2.16 Display Options for Key Figures

There are also some advanced functions that allow individual key figures values and the aggregated results of a key figure to be recalculated locally in the report results. The standard values brought back from the database are overridden by these local calculations. Two examples of these functions include Maximum, which displays the highest key figure value for the characteristic combinations found in the results; and Rank Number, which assigns an integer of 1 to the highest value found and then continues ranking from the largest value down to the smallest. Some of these functions are only supported in Web applications. Table 2.2 summarizes the commonly used key figure calculations.

Calculation Function	Description
Minimum	The system displays the minimum key figure value for a characteristic.
Maximum	The system displays the maximum key figure value for a characteristic.

Table 2.2 Commonly Used Key Figure Calculations

Calculation Function	Description
Moving Average	The system calculates the average of all values.
Normalize According to Overall Result	The data is displayed as a percentage of the overall result. The values of the results row and the overall results row are not displayed as percentages but as absolute values. If there are multiple characteristics in the drilldown, there are different results, which are combined to form an overall result.
Rank	The characteristic values are ranked based on the size of the value, where the largest value has rank 1 and the smallest value has the last rank. If a value occurs more than once, the corresponding characteristic values are assigned the same rank. In a basic ranked list, the next smallest value is assigned this rank incremented by one, for example: Rank 1 = 1000 Rank 2 = 500 Rank 2 = 500 **Rank 3 = 250**
Olympic Rank	The Olympic ranked list differs from the basic ranked list as follows: In the Olympic ranked list, when a value occurs more than once, the next smallest value is not assigned the rank incremented by one, but the rank that corresponds to the number of previous characteristic values, for example: Rank 1 = 1000 Rank 2 = 500 Rank 2 = 500 **Rank 4 = 250**

Table 2.2 Commonly Used Key Figure Calculations (Cont.)

When defining a query definition, you may have to restrict certain characteristics to individual values, or to a range of values; for example, sales data for the month of March, or sales data for a particular set of sales employees.

Characteristics found in a query definition can be restricted to a single value, a range of values, multiple single values, and multiple ranges. To restrict a characteristic, select the Filter pane and right-click on the name of the characteristic found in the *Default Values* or *Characteristic Restriction area* and choose Restrict from the context menu. Alternatively, simply double-click on the name of the characteristic.

The Selection Values dialog opens. The Fixed Values available for the characteristic appear on the left side of the dialog. The Selection area is on the right side of the window (see Figure 2.17). This is where the selections that become restrictions for the query definition will appear. You can add restrictions in one of several ways:

► On the left side, double-click on the item to be restricted.

► Drag and drop the item to be restricted from the left to the right.

► Highlight the item and click on the ADD arrow.

► Search for specific values by using the Search feature.

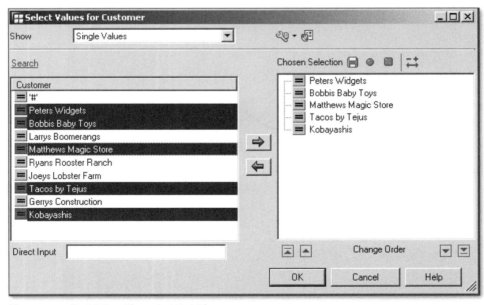

Figure 2.17 Restricting Characteristic Values

To transfer more than one value, hold down the Ctrl key and use one of the afore-mentioned methods to move items from the left to the right. To select a large range of continuous values, change the Show drop-down box from Single Values to Value Range. To define a value range, double-click on the first value and then double-click on the last value.

Occasionally, most of the values for a characteristic are required. When this occurs, it may be easier to simply exclude the values that are not required. Excluding values is accomplished in two steps.

1. Transfer the value to be excluded to the right side of the Selection dialog.

2. Right-click on the selected value and choose Exclude from Selection.

This will change the color associated with the selection icon to red. This exclusion is identified in Figure 2.18. It is also possible to download or upload a list of selections by right-clicking on the Chosen selection side and choosing the appropriate option. Once applied, the inclusion or exclusion will appear in a submenu below the characteristic in the Filter pane.

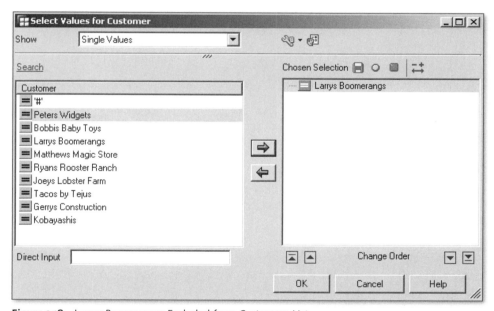

Figure 2.18 Larrys Boomerangs Excluded from Customers List

Sometimes, seeing the keys associated with characteristic values, along with the descriptions, is very useful. To activate the technical names (keys), click on the wrench icon found in the toolbar of the Select Values window. This will add a second column that provides more information, similar to that shown in Figure 2.19. This will help a report designer distinguish between two values with the same or similar descriptions. No two characteristic values can have the same technical name or key.

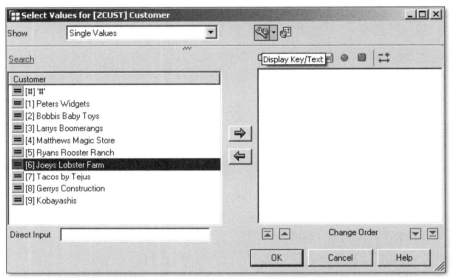

Figure 2.19 Technical Names Help Locate Specific Characteristic Values to be Included or Excluded

2.7 Restricted and Calculated Key Figures

Key figures can also be restricted. To create RKFs, double-click on the name of a key figure in the Columns pane. The Change Selection window opens with the current description and definition of the key figure displayed on the right side. The InfoProvider contents are displayed on the left side of the window. To restrict the key figure, simply drag a characteristic from the left to the right side of the window. Next, double-click on the characteristic and choose the relevant values. A restriction on Revenue is shown in Figure 2.20. This column restriction will only return Revenues for the Cal. Yr/Month of January 2008. For clarity, you can update the column description from "Revenue" to "Revenue for January 2008."

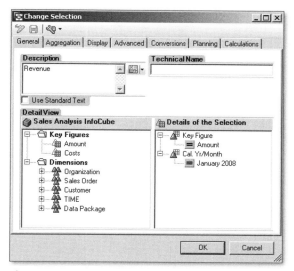

Figure 2.20 Key Figure Revenue Restricted to January 2008

RKFs are most often used to create a series of columns that show data with particular characteristic values.

Repeat the process to create additional RKFs for another Calendar Year/Month.

Using the Copy and Paste functionality (see Figure 2.21) is a way for you to replicate and modify RKF definitions quickly. To copy a restricted key figure, right-click on the key figure's name and choose Copy. Right-click again and choose Paste. Double-click on the copied RKF to change the restriction to February 2008, for example.

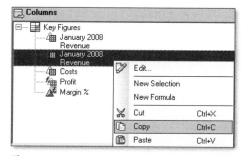

Figure 2.21 Copy and Paste to Create a Quick Series of Restricted Key Figures

InfoProviders contain a fixed number of basic key figures. These key figures can be restricted by using the characteristics found within the different dimensions of an InfoCube. Calculations may also be made on these pre-existing key figures. These CKFs consist of mathematical formulas that use basic key figures, RKFs, and other CKFs as operands. This allows new information to be created.

Many advanced math functions are available. Basic calculator operations such as addition and subtraction, Boolean operators such as "is less than," and data functions such as "if...then" are just some examples. To create a new calculated key figure, right-click on the name of the structure in the Columns pane and select New Formula (see Figure 2.22).

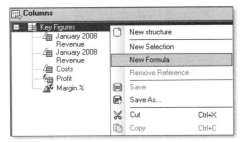

Figure 2.22 Creation of a New Calculated Key Figure

A new Formula key figure will appear in the columns. To construct a formula, either double-click on the new Formula or click on the Edit button found in the Properties pane. All existing basic key figures, RKFs, and CKFs are listed in the Available Operands section. Predefined math functions are located in the Operators section and basic mathematical symbols are listed horizontally above these two sections. A name must be assigned to this new CKF by entering a description that replaces the default Formula description. Constructing a new formula can be as simple as selecting an operand, an operator/function, and a second operand. Common CKFs are variance formulas that calculate the difference between an actual value and a budgeted value.

Once a formula has been created, the display settings for the CKF can be adjusted by using the Display tab found in the Change Formula window or in the Properties pane.

Frequently, a CKF will have a formula that is syntactically correct, but not logically correct. For example, a report developer could have inadvertently created a new CKF called "Revenue Variance" with the formula:

```
Revenue Variance = Actuals — Actuals
```

This formula would pass the syntax check. However, you'll notice that a simple typo on the variance formula would not be flagged by the BEx Query Designer messages pane. This is a logic error, and the danger here is that this formula could be shared with many users if this report is published to a role or distributed using the BEx Broadcaster. Therefore, it is critical that you check all CKFs and RKFs carefully to ensure that their descriptions align with the underlying formula both logically and syntactically.

2.8   Advanced Calculations

Defining more advanced formulas for CKFs extends the value of the data found within an InfoProvider. These calculations enable you to make further conclusions that would otherwise go unanswered. Some of the more frequently used mathematical functions are listed and described in Table 2.3.

Function	Syntax	Description
Percentage Variance	<Operand A> % <Operand B>	This gives the percentage variance between the two operands.
Percentage Share	<Operand A> %A <Operand B>	Expresses the percentage share of key figure A and key figure B.
Value without Dimensions (without Units)	NODIM (<Operand>)	Hides units and currencies leaving just the values.
Absolute Value	ABS (<Operand>)	Removes the positive or negative sign from the values.
No Error (x)	NOERR (<Operand>)	Avoids error messages by returning a value of zero instead of an arithmetic error for undefined calculations or arithmetic errors.

Table 2.3 Frequently Used Mathematical Functions

Function	Syntax	Description
Boolean Operators < , <=, <>, ==, >, >=	<Expression A> <Boolean Operator> <Expression B>	Results in a value of 1 if the statement is true, otherwise it returns a value of 0.
Logical AND	<Expression A> AND <Expression B>	Returns a value of 1 if both expression A and B are true, otherwise returns 0.

Table 2.3 Frequently Used Mathematical Functions (Cont.)

2.9   Using Structures

Creating a series of key figures, RKFs, and CKFs for a query definition takes time. An efficient way of reusing a collection of key figures that have been formatted, restricted, and extended with calculations is to save them back to the InfoProvider. Structures can save the current configuration of objects in either the Columns pane or the Rows pane.

To save your work as a reusable structure, right-click on Key Figures in the Columns pane or on Structure in the Rows pane of your query definition and choose Save As. The pop-up window Save Structure As opens and prompts you for a technical name and a description of the structure. There is no standard naming convention; however, most companies have instituted the common practice of starting the technical names of any user-developed objects with a Y or Z. Enter a technical name and an appropriate description for the structure. After you click OK, the structure is saved back to the InfoProvider and stored in the Structure folder. The new description for the saved structure will now appear in the query definition.

New queries have only one structure by default, which is located in the Columns pane. This Column structure is created as soon as one key figure is added to the columns. If you start with a blank query and then add a key figure to the Rows pane, you'll create a structure called Key Figures. You can create a second structure in the Rows column, but it is generated differently; that is, you cannot create a second structure by dragging and dropping characteristics to the Rows pane. Instead, you must right-click on the label for the Rows pane and choose New Structure (see Figure 2.23).

Figure 2.23 Creating a New Structure in the Rows Pane

This structure will now appear at the top of the Rows pane. You can add objects to the Rows structure by following the menu path STRUCTURE • NEW SELECTION (see Figure 2.24). Creating a restricted selection as a row is similar to creating an RKF in the columns except that you do not need to include a key figure—you can simply restrict values of multiple characteristics across one row in the report.

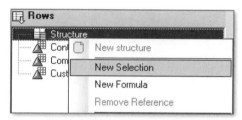

Figure 2.24 Creating a New Selection for a Rows Structure

Each selection in a Rows structure allows you to define a combination of characteristics within it. For that reason, you should give each new selection an appropriate description that explains the logic defined for that row. For example, you might combine a particular customer with a specific date range for a new selection created within a structure.

Rows structures allow combinations of characteristics to be defined for a single line in the output of a report. A sample element for a Rows structure is shown in Figure 2.25.

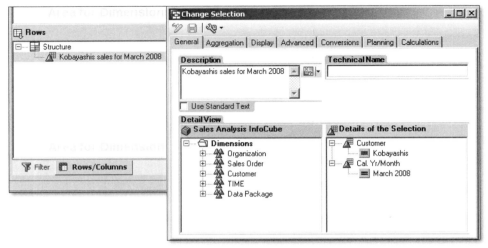

Figure 2.25 Sample Rows Structure

2.10   Creating Fixed Query Dimensions

You can create reports in SAP BI that have a fixed number of rows and columns. This is ideal for operational reporting where the requirements are well known and the data components that make up the report never change. Creating financial statements, such as an income statements or balance sheets, with fixed dimensions allows for additional formatting and referencing options. Furthermore, being able to predict the exact cell reference within a BEx Analyzer report in which a particular value will appear lets report developers use Excel cell referencing and construct custom reports by pulling data from more than one fixed dimension report. Fixed dimension reports are created by leveraging the capabilities of structures. Defining a fixed number of rows using a Rows structure, along with a fixed number of columns in a Columns structure, results in a predictable matrix that can also prove accommodating. These reports can be optimized for presentation and printing as the dimensions are always the same. Queries that are fixed in dimensions by only utilizing Rows and Columns structure elements also meet the prerequisites for using the BEx Report Designer, which allows for presentation quality formatting of a query definition containing two structures.

2.11   Using Characteristic Variables

Creating restrictions for characteristics in a query definition limits the data that is displayed in the output of a report. An alternative to hard coding a restriction for a characteristic is to use a variable instead. Variables are empty placeholders that get populated when a user executes a query.

Variables build much-needed flexibility into reports, and therefore can make the same report more usable for many more users. By employing a user-entry variable for the characteristic Calendar Year/Period, a single report can serve many requests. Variables can be processed in different ways; however, the most common approach is to use characteristic value variables that allow users to select a value(s) at run-time. Variables are created within the BEx Query Designer. Preexisting characteristic value variables reside within a submenu for each characteristic that is found under the dimensions of an InfoProvider (see Figure 2.26). To check the properties of an existing variable, simply double-click on it. The characteristic variable definition window is shown in Figure 2.27. If an appropriately defined variable does not exist for a particular requirement a new one can be easily created.

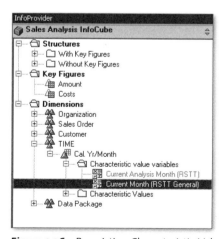

Figure 2.26   Preexisting Characteristic Value Variables Folder

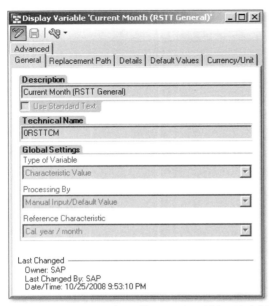

Figure 2.27 Settings for a Characteristic Value Variable

New variables can be constructed without programming. You can create a new user-entry variable by right-clicking on the Characteristic value variables icon displayed below a characteristic on the InfoProvider side of the Query Designer. A New Variable appears and needs to be configured by a set of parameters. Double-click on the New Variable to define these parameters. Similar to a structure, a variable requires a description and a technical name. When you enter a Variable Name, ensure that you adhere to the naming conventions for your organization. The Description for the variable should contain enough information so that the user running the report knows the purpose of the variable. Enter a Technical Name and a Description and highlight the General tab as shown in Figure 2.28. The General tab defines how the variable will be processed—in this case by User Entry or Manual Input. It also defines the reference characteristic—in this case Cal. Yr/Month.

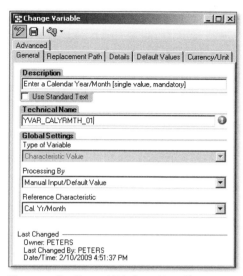

Figure 2.28 General Tab for a New Characteristics Value Variable

The Details tab (see Figure 2.29) allows the variable to be represented in several different ways. A variable can serve as a placeholder for:

▸ A Single Value (only one value can be chosen)

▸ Multiple Single Values (more than one value can be selected)

▸ Interval (a single range of values)

▸ Selection Option (allows for multiple values or multiple ranges)

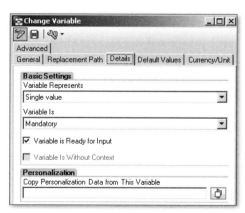

Figure 2.29 Details Tab of the Change Variable Window

You can also designate a variable as optional. When a variable entry is optional, a user does not have to make a selection when the query is executed. When a variable entry is mandatory, the query cannot be executed until a user makes a selection. In this case the variable will be mandatory and only allow a user to enter one value for Calendar Year/Month at a time—thereby restricting the amount of data that can be requested and improving performance for this particular query.

Other features and options are possible using the remaining tabs, but they aren't required to finish creating a new characteristic variable. To finish creating a new characteristic value variable, click the Save variable icon found in the top toolbar of the Change Variable window. This will save the variable back to the InfoProvider and make it available under the characteristic value variable folder (see Figure 2.30) for that particular characteristic—in this case Cal. Yr/Month.

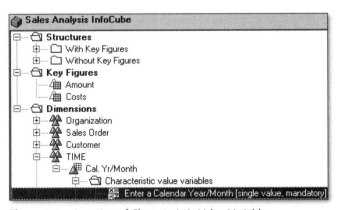

Figure 2.30   Location of Characteristic Value Variables

Once a characteristic variable has been saved you can modify certain elements of a variable later, such as the Description, but some details (the way the variable is represented as a Single Value, for example) cannot be changed.

When a query containing variables is executed, the pop-up window, displayed in Figure 2.31, allows users to interact with the report and select a value(s).

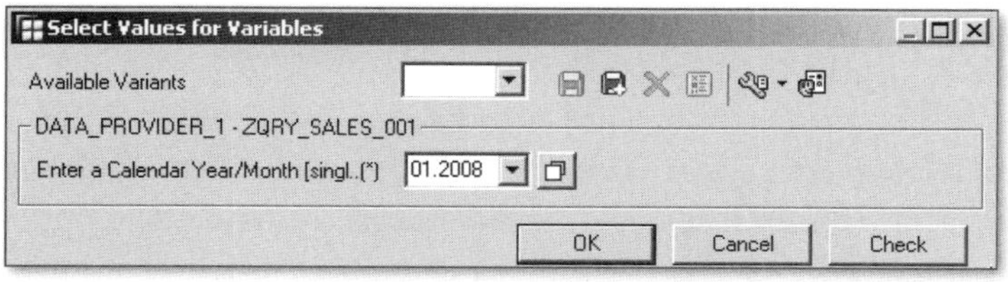

Figure 2.31 The Variable Screen Allows Users to Make Selections at Runtime

The number of variables for a single characteristic can grow substantially, especially when a company has many report developers. Therefore, you should always check the preexisting characteristic variables before you create new ones.

> **Tip**
>
> Another feature of characteristic value variables is offsets. You can use variable offsets to increase or decrease a selected value by a fixed number of units. A variable for the fiscal year can prompt a user to enter a year, and this year can be used to restrict an Actuals column. This same input can then be used in a subsequent Actuals column for the prior year (an offset of –1).

Variable offsets are defined by double-clicking on a variable used in an RKF. Locate an RKF definition that deploys a characteristic value variable and double-click on the variable itself. To offset a user entry, right-click on the variable and choose Set Offset for Variable from the context menu or use the –/+ icon found in the same pop-up window shown in Figure 2.32. The Set Variable Offset screen allows users to enter positive or negative integers. An offset of –1 changes the relative value of a user-defined input to one logical unit less than what was entered by the user. If a user enters a Cal. Yr/Month of January 2009, the key figure, which deploys a variable offset of –1, will reflect data for December 2008.

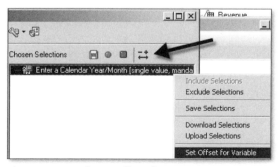

Figure 2.32 Defining Offsets for User Entry Variables

2.12   Creating Exceptions

Exceptions highlight certain values or thresholds indicated within the data of a report. Exceptions are defined using the Exceptions icon in the BEx Query Designer toolbar. After clicking on the Exceptions icon, a new Exceptions pane will appear in the Query Designer. Right-click on the blank area and choose New Exception. A new Exception 1 is ready to be defined. Double-click on Exception 1 to define the parameters. The Change Exception window is shown in Figure 2.33. Highlighting is accomplished with nine different color ranges. Exceptions are defined for particular key figures. If a key figure value falls within a predefined range, that value is highlighted with the assigned color.

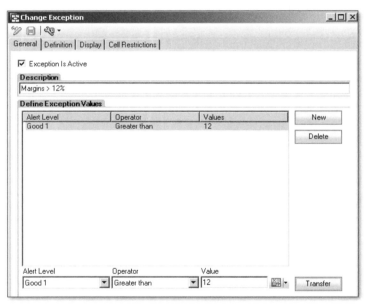

Figure 2.33   Exception Defined for Margins > 12%

Figure 2.34 illustrates the output of the exception that was defined for the sample report used throughout this chapter. Only values for Margins that exceed 12% are highlighted using the Good 1 threshold, which color codes values in green.

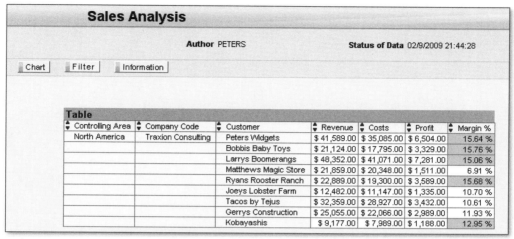

Figure 2.34 An Exception Applied Against a Key Figure for Margin %

Exceptions work very well with reports that have a large dataset. Being able to eye-ball the results quickly on screen and focus in on values that are "Red" or "Yellow" is highly efficient. Exceptions can be applied to the individual values that appear in a column, to only the subtotals or results rows, or both.

Exceptions are easy to construct and are defined from a single pop-up window within the Query Designer, requiring zero programming knowledge. Before you can create an exception, you should indentify the following:

▶ A key figure or structure row to analyze

▶ A threshold value or value range to focus on

▶ A color or alert level to assign

▶ A description for the exception definition

The alert levels are assigned a color that represents a measure of success that mirrors traffic lights. Greens are measured as good, yellows as medium, and reds as bad. There are three shades to each measure of success, for example, Good 1, Good 2, and Good 3 are all shades of green that blend toward yellow. The rainbow of available colors is shown in Figure 2.35.

Sales Volume
1,500,000.00
1,336,330.00
917,678.00
897,392.58
660,671.00
583,679.01
374,893.08
353,121.68
336,133.03
307,362.36
244,490.23
179,759.24
110,077.97
52,669.99
17,547.76
571.00
0.00

Figure 2.35 Results of an Exception with Nine Different Exception Ranges

When defining an exception, you should determine whether a color or alert level should be visible by default when a query is executed, or whether a report user can activate it later on. This can be set with the Exception is Active checkbox in the Change Exception. By default, this checkbox is turned on, meaning the exception will be active when the initial view of the results appears. Exceptions can be toggled on and off while navigating a report.

When many overlapping exception ranges are defined, the SAP BI system selects the threshold that is more conservative, that is, less optimistic. Examples include:

▶ An exception range of 10–20 is red.

▶ An exception range of 20–30 is yellow.

▶ An exception range of 30–40 is green.

▶ A value of exactly 20 found in the report is red.

▶ A value of 30 found in the report is yellow.

You can also define exceptions dynamically. Instead of predefining fixed ranges for each color, exception variables can prompt users to enter their own value ranges at runtime. To define exceptions so they behave this way, use the Exception Variable creation icon that appears next to the Transfer button in the Change Exception screen. A single query definition can have many exceptions created against it. This allows for multiple business or what-if scenarios to be assessed. Each exception can be toggled on/off during navigation by a user whether done through the BEx Analyzer or through a BEx Web Application.

2.13 Creating Conditions

Conditions allow a user to analyze data quickly. Similar to exceptions, conditions highlight data that meets a certain threshold. Also, like exceptions, conditions can be turned on or off while looking at the output of a report. Instead of color-coding specific values or value ranges, conditions *eliminate* any data that does not meet the specific requirements outlined in the condition. For this reason, it is highly recommend that you set conditions to be inactive by default.

Conditions are defined using the Conditions icon in the BEx Query Designer toolbar. After clicking on the Conditions icon a new Conditions pane will appear in the Query Designer. Right-click on the blank area and choose New Condition. A new Condition 1 is ready to be defined. Double-click on Condition 1 to define the parameters. You can also call the Conditions editor using the Edit button found in the Properties pane. Conditions are defined for a particular key figure or structure element. The Change Condition window is shown in Figure 2.36. Conditions allow the use of mathematical operators, which add additional logic to the filtering criteria.

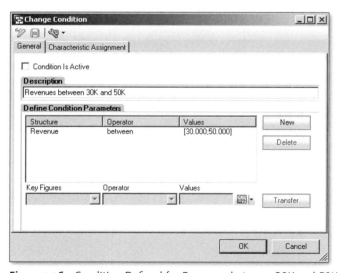

Figure 2.36 Condition Defined for Revenues between 30K and 50K

Some common operators used in defining conditions are:

► Greater than/Less than

► Between (a range of values)

► Top N (only shows the largest N values from a data set)

► Bottom % (only shows the bottom N% of values from a data set)

> **Tip**
>
> When conditions are created for a query, a new tab appears in the middle of the Query Designer called Conditions (shown in Figure 2.37). The same is true for exceptions that are created against a query definition.

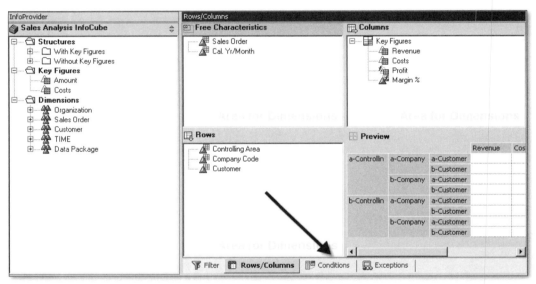

Figure 2.37   Tabs in the Query Designer Allow Easy Access to Conditions and Exceptions

2.14   Query Properties

The Query Properties icon in the BEx Query Designer toolbar allows for certain formatting and display options to be assigned to the overall query definition.

The General tab allows for changes to the title or description of a report.

The Variable Sequence tab allows a report developer to change the sequence or order of user-entry variables that appear when the query is executed. For example, it may be helpful to have all of the mandatory variables listed first (if applicable).

The Display tab has the option to Hide Repeated Key Values. This setting is active by default and specifies whether identical characteristic values are to be displayed more than once in a query. Display Scaling Factors for Key Figures adds an additional column header that provides information about any numbers that have been scaled (i.e., *1000). In addition, key figures typically have units or a currency associated to every value. Setting Display Scaling Factors for Key Figures to active also has the side effect of putting the units/currency for a key figure into the column header at the top, instead of displaying it on each number going down the page.

The Rows/Columns tab lets a report designer specify where the results are displayed: above/below the rows and left/right of the columns. There are also options for Suppressing Zeros, which specify how to handle rows or columns that are filled with zeros.

The choices are:

▶ Do Not Suppress—zeros are always displayed.

▶ Active—any Columns/Rows with a resulting value of zero are not displayed. See Figure 2.38 for an example.

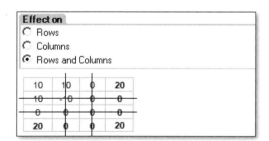

Figure 2.38 Example of Active Zero Suppression

▶ Active (All Values = 0)—Columns/Rows containing all zeros are not displayed. See Figure 2.39 for an example.

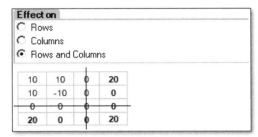

Figure 2.39 Example of Active (All Values = 0) Suppression

The Value Display tab provides options for how to handle negative values with the minus sign:

▶ Before the Number –123.45. This is the default setting.

▶ After the Number 123.45–

▶ In Parentheses (123.45):

The Value Display tab also provides options for how to handle the display of values equal to 0. The available options are zeros:

▶ with currency/unit. This is the default setting i.e., 100 USD

▶ without currency/unit: zeros i.e., 100

▶ as a space; cells containing a zero become blank

▶ as default text; user-defined text is displayed instead of zeros

The Planning tab determines whether the query definition is started in display or change mode. This is only active for input-ready queries that allow a user to manually enter planning data at runtime using Integrated Planning (IP).

The Advanced tab allows a query definition to be used as an external data source. Checking the box next to Allow External Access to this Query will make it available to third-party tools, such as Crystal Reports.

2.15   Errors, Messages, and Help

The error-handling concept in Query Designer allows you to create and edit a query and query objects without disrupting your individual workflow. The BEx Query Designer informs a user of errors by underlining incomplete or erroneous objects in red. However, your work will not be disrupted by pop-up messages appearing each time. Instead, error messages are displayed in the Messages pane instead. Warnings and information are also displayed here. The messages are displayed in groups for more clarity. They are displayed in the following categories, which you can expand and collapse as needed:

▸ Messages for the current query

▸ Messages about server elements that were loaded for use in the query

▸ Status messages

For example, when a new exception is called and it has yet to be configured, it is underlined in red and appropriate warning messages appear in the Messages pane advising a query designer to take action (see Figure 2.40).

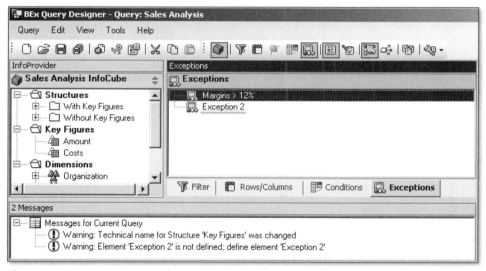

Figure 2.40 Warning Messages for an Incomplete Exception Definition

When presented with these errors, the simplest way to address them is by right-clicking on the erroneous object and choosing the menu path: ERROR HELP • EXPLAIN THIS ERROR. A new Documents pane will appear in the middle of the Query Designer tool and provide context-sensitive information on how to address the situation as shown in Figure 2.41. A separate menu path from the Error Help context menu is ERROR HELP • POSSIBLE CORRECTIONS, which takes a query designer to the only possible options that will correct the error. Usually, an error can be resolved very quickly. Report developers can also access the entire SAP help library for the Query Designer by clicking on the Help button found on the menu bar and choosing Application Help or simply pushing ⌐F1⌐. Lastly, if necessary, a designer who is more comfortable with the previous BW 3.x version of the BEx Query Designer can revert to it by clicking on the View button found on the menu bar and follow the menu path Predefined • SAP BW 3.x View.

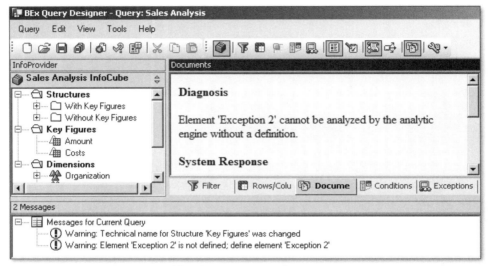

Figure 2.41 Context Sensitive Held in the Documents Tab

2.16 Summary

The BEx Query Designer makes it easy to create and design flexible query definitions that can be used by a wide variety of users. When designing queries, you should focus on performance and usability. By inserting many characteristics to the Rows and Free Characteristics panes, users are empowered with much more informational freedom to add and remove data at their leisure. The trade-off, however, is performance.

Inserting more and more objects to a query definition results in longer wait times for users. On the other hand, it is impractical to create completely inflexible queries that accommodate only one end user. This approach results in a maintenance headache where many query definitions have to be maintained and updated by power users or Information Technology (IT). The optimal approach requires a query-to-user ratio that is much greater than 1:1, but not so large a ratio that there is a significant degradation of performance for users who are looking for quick answers. The balance between performance and usability is an issue that escapes no SAP BI implementation. The system hardware, data model, data volumes, performance tuning, reporting requirements, and user expectations make the solution to this hotly debated topic unique to each and every organization.

3   Creating High-Impact Workbooks

The Business Explorer (BEx) Analyzer is the primary reporting environment for SAP NetWeaver Business Intelligence (BI) users. Your reports will have more use and greater acceptance by stretching the capabilities of this tool. This chapter will help you create your own high-impact workbooks using the BEx Analyzer. The BEx Analyzer uses an add-in with Microsoft (MS) Excel. It is shown as part of the BEx Suite in Figure 3.1.

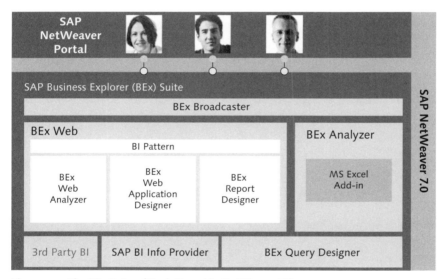

Figure 3.1   The BEx Suite of Tools Found in NetWeaver 7.0

3.1   Overview of the BEx Analyzer

The BEx Analyzer is the SAP BI reporting tool embedded within Excel. SAP NetWeaver BI 7.0 provides enhanced navigation features, such as drag and drop to facilitate end-user interaction, a new design mode to develop applications, and additional integration with Excel formatting and formulas. In addition, the Integrated Planning (IP) tool allows planning to be done using BEx Analyzer workbooks. Users can also employ Visual Basic Applications (VBA) to add customized programming capabilities. When launching the BEx Analyzer, two SAP toolbars are added to the standard MS Excel environment (see Figure 3.2). To access data, users must log on to their SAP instance and open an existing query, workbook, or query view. In the BEx Analyzer, you can analyze data by navigating within the context menu. Online Analytical Processing (OLAP) functionality such as filtering, sorting, and using drilldowns can all be done from the SAP BI BEx Analyzer toolbar. Users can also leverage Excel functionality to create new formulas or formatting for the report output.

Figure 3.2 SAP BI BEx Analyzer Toolbars

As of SAP NetWeaver BI 7.0 the BEx Analyzer's functionality is divided into two modes, each with a dedicated toolbar. The Analysis mode, which uses the Analysis toolbar, is for performing OLAP analysis on queries. The Design mode, which uses the Design toolbar, allows a user to design a custom interface for query applications. The Analysis toolbar consists of the following icons in the order in which they appear:

► Open

► Save

► Refresh/Pause Automatic Refresh

► Change Variable Values

► Tools

► Global Settings

► System Information

► Application Help

The Design toolbar consists of the following icons in the order in which they appear:

► Design Mode/Exit Design Mode

► Insert Analysis Grid

- ▶ Insert Navigation Pane
- ▶ Insert List of Filters
- ▶ Insert Button
- ▶ Insert Dropdown Box
- ▶ Insert Checkbox Group
- ▶ Insert Radio Button Group
- ▶ Insert List of Conditions
- ▶ Insert List of Exceptions
- ▶ Insert Text
- ▶ Insert Messages
- ▶ Workbook Settings

The Analysis toolbar is used when navigating data. The BEx Analyzer has a standard workbook design that consists of an analysis grid (the table of results), a Navigation pane, a series of text fields found in an information box, and two additional text fields — Author and Status of Data. Lastly, there is a button that converts the table to a graphical chart. The Design toolbar largely goes unused with most users as the standard SAP workbook template is sufficient for most purposes. Power users may find limitations with the standard template and want to create their own customized versions. Creating new templates is covered later in this chapter.

3.2 Integration with MS Excel

The BEx Analyzer enables you to access any of the native MS Excel functionality along with the SAP BI functionality. As you'll see, having two tools in a single environment can be quite powerful.

A user can execute a query definition into the BEx Analyzer tool. The data is embedded into an MS Excel worksheet. A user can filter a specific characteristic value by double-clicking on it. This takes advantage of the BI OLAP engine. Alternatively, a user can turn on Excel's AutoFilter tool and it will automatically pick up the correct column headings from your BI report.

3.3 Using the BEx Analyzer

Executing a query in the BEx Analyzer is as easy as opening word processor documents or spreadsheets. Launch the BEx Analyzer within a Windows Start menu and use the menu path START • PROGRAMS • BUSINESS EXPLORER • ANALYZER.

After Excel launches, a Security Warning dialog regarding macros may appear. To ensure that the BI functionality works properly, you must enable macros (click on Enable Macros). The BEx toolbars will appear within an Excel window. To locate and execute an existing query, click on the Open icon found in the Analysis toolbar and choose Queries.

When attempting to open a query, the BEx Analyzer will prompt a user to log on to a specific BI system. From the SAP Logon window, select the appropriate BI environment and click OK. Then, log on to the BI environment by entering the correct Client, User ID, Password, and Language. Click OK to continue.

A pop-up window opens, displaying all of the available queries that a user can access. Queries are located under public folders called Roles, or listed within private folders called Favorites. Queries can also be searched for using the Find functionality or systematically located by navigating through the available InfoProviders found under the InfoAreas button. Once located, highlight a query and click Open. When the query finishes executing, the data will be embedded within a worksheet. The default view of the query definition will appear. An example is provided in Figure 3.3.

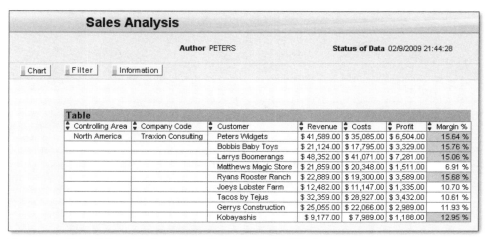

Figure 3.3 Default Template for a Query Definition in the BEx Analyzer

The BEx Analyzer tool provides typical functions for modifying data such as selecting, refreshing, saving, and formatting a query. The query definition determines the initial view of the query. Once executed, a query is embedded into a worksheet with standard BI formatting. There are four sections to every query that become embedded into the standard BEx Analyzer template. These are:

► Title

► Navigation pane

► Text elements

► Analysis grid

The *title* of the query is defined by the query definition properties. The title of the query displayed in Figure 3.3 is Sales Analysis. The *Navigation pane* lists the characteristics and free characteristics included within a *query* and allows for them to be added to the *results*, or filtered via the context menu. The Navigation pane is accessed by clicking on the Filter button found in the standard BEx Analyzer template (see Figure 3.3). Text elements provide housekeeping information on a query such as when it was created, who created it, and when it was last changed. These Text Elements are made visible by clicking on the Information button found in the standard BEx Analyzer template. A sample of some common text elements is shown in Figure 3.4.

Information			
Author	PETERS	Last Refreshed	02/11/2009 17:25:03
Current User	PETERS	Key Date	02/11/2009
Last Changed By	PETERS	Changed At	02/10/2009 18:36:00
InfoProvider	ZCSALES	Status of Data	02/9/2009 21:44:28
Query Technical Name	ZQRY_SALES_001	Relevance of Data (Date)	02/9/2009
Query Description	Sales Analysis	Relevance of Data (Time)	1:44:28

Figure 3.4 Text Elements Found under the Information Heading

One particularly useful text element is *Status of Data*, which provides the date and time that the InfoProvider was last updated. This can be extremely helpful when you're trying to determine the relevancy of data in a report. For example, a query may be executed on March 30, but the Status of Data text element displays March 15. Therefore, by just reading this text element, a user knows that the underlying BI data was last updated on March 15. Business transactions from March 15 to March 30 may not be reflected in the query results.

The analysis grid is simply a table of data that is returned as a result of executing a query. The analysis grid provides the main analysis functions in the BEx Analyzer. A user can navigate and execute OLAP functions directly on the analysis grid by either using the context menu when right-clicking or by dragging items from the Navigation pane and dropping them on the analysis grid. The context menu functions that are available for various cell types are summarized in Table 3.1.

Context Menu Function	Behavior
Back One Navigation Step	Restores the previous navigational state allowing a user to undo a step.
Back to Start	Returns the workbook to the initial query view when the workbook was originally opened.
Convert to Formula	A function that converts the data found in cells into individual formulas that can be manipulated using Excel.
Select Filter Value	Presents a dialog box where a user can apply simple or complex filter selections.
Remove Filter	Removes a previously selected filter and displays all values.

Table 3.1 Summary of Context Menu Functions

Context Menu Function	Behavior
Swap....with...	Exchanges the relative location of two different characteristics.
Drill Down in Columns	Spreads the selected characteristic of structure member across the key figures found in the analysis grid.
Remove Drilldown	Removes the selected characteristic from the analysis grid.
Swap Axes	Switches the relative position of the rows and columns.
Properties	Presents a dialog box for characteristic properties if called from a characteristic cell. Presents the key figures properties dialog if executed from a key figure cell.
Query Properties	Calls the Query Properties dialog, where global query properties found in the workbook can be modified.
Goto	Leverages any Report-Report-Interfacing (RRI) that has been previously defined for the query definition. Also referred to as jump targets.
Create Condition	Allows a user to create and edit existing conditions.

Table 3.1 Summary of Context Menu Functions (Cont.)

In addition to the Context Menu, a user can perform many navigation functions by double-clicking the mouse. By double-clicking on a characteristic found in the Navigation pane, a user can quickly add a drill-down to the report. If a characteristic is already in the analysis grid, double-clicking removes the information from the display. Double-clicking on the value of a cell found in the results area applies a filter based on that particular characteristic value. For example, if a Cost Center of 12345 is found in the analysis grid, simply clicking on it will remove all of the other Cost Centers and keep 12345 as the Cost Center of interest in the results. This filter is displayed under the corresponding characteristic listed in the Navigation pane.

A new BEx Analyzer feature delivered with BI 7.0 is the ability to enter filter values directly into the Navigation pane. Prior to this latest release a user would have to follow the Context Menu to filter on multiple values. This new function allows characteristic values to be entered manually, using commas to separate single values. Knowing the key values for individual accounts, customers, or products would allow a user to enter these directly against the corresponding characteristic in the navigation block.

The BEx Analyzer provides another very useful function that extracts individual subreports from a larger query. As an example, look at the demo query found in Figure 3.5. This query, now embedded into the BEx Analyzer as a worksheet, displays customer revenues, costs, profit, and margin percentage. Notice that a characteristic called Calendar Year/Month (Cal. Yr/Month) is found in the Navigation pane. In a typical scenario it may be of value to create separate worksheets that show sales results by month. This would normally be quite a bit of work to copy and paste results into different worksheets to produce the desired output.

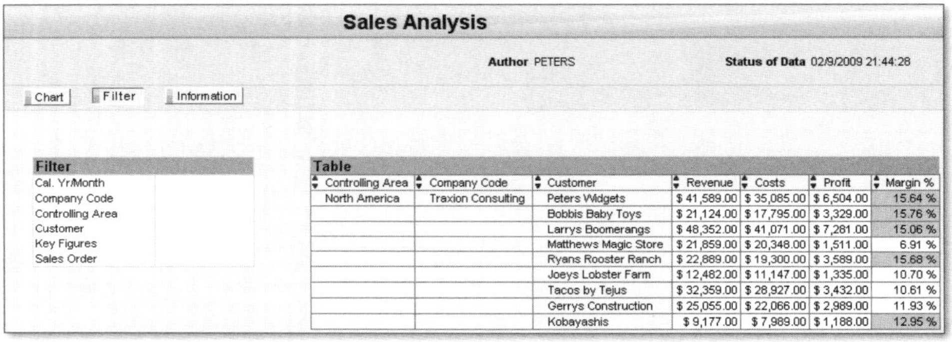

Sales Analysis

| | | | Author PETERS | | | | Status of Data 02/9/2009 21:44:28 |

Chart | Filter | Information

Filter

Table						
Controlling Area	Company Code	Customer	Revenue	Costs	Profit	Margin %
North America	Traxion Consulting	Peters Widgets	$ 41,589.00	$ 35,085.00	$ 6,504.00	15.64 %
		Bobbis Baby Toys	$ 21,124.00	$ 17,795.00	$ 3,329.00	15.76 %
		Larrys Boomerangs	$ 48,352.00	$ 41,071.00	$ 7,281.00	15.06 %
		Matthews Magic Store	$ 21,859.00	$ 20,348.00	$ 1,511.00	6.91 %
		Ryans Rooster Ranch	$ 22,889.00	$ 19,300.00	$ 3,589.00	15.68 %
		Joeys Lobster Farm	$ 12,482.00	$ 11,147.00	$ 1,335.00	10.70 %
		Tacos by Tejus	$ 32,359.00	$ 28,927.00	$ 3,432.00	10.61 %
		Gerrys Construction	$ 25,055.00	$ 22,066.00	$ 2,989.00	11.93 %
		Kobayashis	$ 9,177.00	$ 7,989.00	$ 1,188.00	12.95 %

Filter list:
Cal. Yr/Month
Company Code
Controlling Area
Customer
Key Figures
Sales Order

Figure 3.5 The Free Characteristic Cal.Yr/Month is Found in the Navigation Pane

To break up the query results into separate worksheets by Calendar Year/Month, a user can right-click on Cal. Yr/Month, found in the Filter pane, and choose Add Drilldown According to Cal. Yr/Month in New Worksheets. This function generates a new worksheet for each Calendar Year/Month of data that is recorded in the InfoCube that the query is based on. In this example there were 12 Calendar Year/Months. The results workbook now has the original Sales Analysis report for the entire year, plus separate results for each month. Figure 3.6 displays the final result. Notice how only results for November 2008 are displayed on the highlighted worksheet.

Similarly to the BEx Query Designer, which is mostly used by power users, the BEx Analyzer allows end users to create their own local Conditions. In Analysis mode, right-click on the analysis grid and choose Query Properties. Select the Conditions tab and again, right-click in the blank area to choose Create. In the Condition window, right-click a third time on the blank space and choose New to define the Condition parameters. Use the Characteristic Assignment tab to focus in on a specific combination of characteristics to evaluate against, if required. When finished click on OK to return to the worksheet. An example is shown in Figure 3.7.

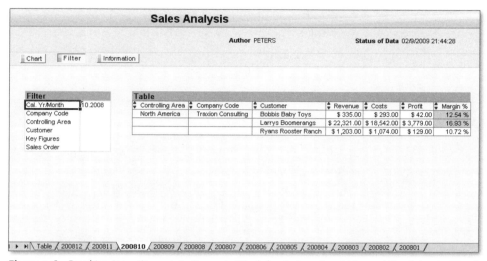

Figure 3.6 Breaking Up a Query into Separate Worksheets Based on Values of the Calendar Year/ Month Characteristic

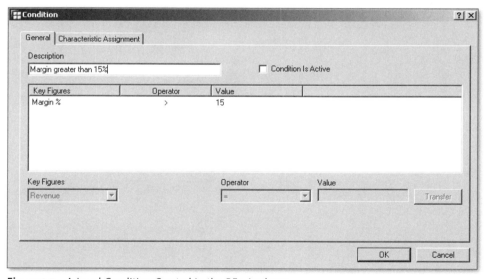

Figure 3.7 A Local Condition Created in the BEx Analyzer

Once created, local conditions are available via the context menu when a user right-clicks on the relevant cell of the analysis grid. Conditions that were created globally using the Query Designer can be turned on or off by navigation, however, the actual definition for these global conditions cannot be adjusted locally using the BEx Analyzer. In this fashion, a power user can safely create conditions that represent corporate thresholds and make these available to all end users. End users, in turn, can create their own local conditions to complete further analysis as needed.

3.4   Creating Custom Templates

The standard BI workbook template has a blue color scheme and a layout that follows the four-section format highlighted in Figure 3.8. One easy way to create more dynamic workbooks is to change the standard template. A custom template, which is assigned to a workbook when the query is executed, can consist of additional graphics, texts, formatting and BEx Design items found in the BEx Design toolbar.

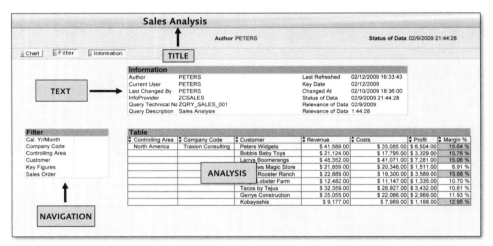

Figure 3.8   Standard BEx Analyzer Template

You can also modify color schemes, visible toolbars, and gridlines using Excel-specific parameters. A template is nothing more than an empty workbook with some formatting. Templates are saved as Excel workbooks and stored on the BI server. Each BI report is then assigned a workbook template, which loads before the query. Using templates allows you to establish a common look and feel to a series of reports, and furthermore, it's quite easy to do. To be set as the default workbook, a template must be stored on the BI server and opened from the server. There is a default workbook assigned for each user. If a user does not create or select a default workbook, the standard BEx Analyzer workbook is used.

Some commonly used Excel functions used to format a template include:

▶ Add images or graphics to the worksheet

▶ Insert additional worksheets to the workbook

▶ Insert a new background image

▶ Created custom VBA code and embed a VBA macro

▶ Format cells with text, borders, and a customized color scheme

Some commonly used BEx Analyzer functions include:

▶ Insert design items from the BEx Design toolbar

▶ Adjust the location of design items

▶ Apply a BEx theme

The following steps show you how to create a custom template within the BEx Analyzer, and how to configure the BI system to a custom template as the default. This exercise assumes the user is using MS Excel 2003. Using a different version may require slightly different selections using the Excel menu paths. During the exercise you will be prompted to log in to a BI system. Have your login ID and password available.

1. Launch the BEx Analyzer.

2. Enable macros if you receive a security warning as shown in Figure 3.9.

Figure 3.9 Macros Enabled for SAP BI to Function Properly

3. Create a new workbook using the MS Excel menu path FILE • NEW. A new workbook opens.

4. Click on cell A1 and insert the text title *My BI Reports Template*. Make the font bold and use a type size of 20.

5. Using the Excel menu, select format • sheet • background.

6. Locate a picture to use as a new background image.

7. Using the Excel menu, select INSERT • PICTURE • CLIP ART.

8. Scroll through the available artwork and double-click on an image to select it.

9. Use the handles to resize the picture so that it appears somewhere in the top left, below the title, and does not go below row 8 of the spreadsheet.

10. Using the Excel menu, select TOOLS • OPTIONS • VIEW. In the Window options section, deactivate the Gridlines checkbox (see Figure 3.10).

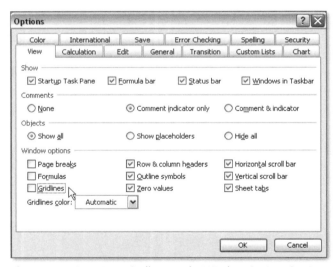

Figure 3.10   Deactivate Gridlines in the Window Options Section

11. Highlight row 8 by clicking on the row header at the left edge of the worksheet.

12. Click on the Borders icon in the Excel Formatting toolbar, and then click on the arrow next to the icon to select a Thick Bottom Border.

Your template should resemble the one shown in Figure 3.11.

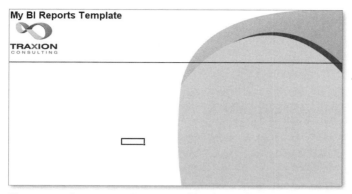

Figure 3.11 Designing a Custom Workbook Template

The look and feel of this template is quite different from the default. The next step is to position placeholders for BEx Design items. These placeholders are populated by a query (Data Provider) after a query is executed. Continue working with the custom template by completing the following steps:

1. Click on cell B11 to make it active. Using the BEx Design toolbar, select the Insert Navigation Pane icon.

2. Click on cell F11 to make it active. Using the BEx Design toolbar, select the Insert Analysis Grid icon.

3. Using the BEx Analysis toolbar, follow the menu path save • save workbook…

4. Enter a description of My Template and Click OK to save this new design to the BI server.

The final template should resemble the one shown in Figure 3.12

Figure 3.12 A Custom Workbook Template with BEx Item Placeholders

A custom template has now been created and saved to the BI server. This template will be used for a specific query — the Sales Analysis query. The Sales Analysis query, also called a Data Provider, needs to be linked to the placeholders representing the analysis grid and Navigation pane. Perform the following steps:

1. Ensure the Design mode is active by clicking on the left-most icon found in the BEx Design toolbar.

2. Click on the placeholder for the Navigation pane found in cell B11. Choose the New icon next to the DataProvider box. Click on the Assign Query/Query View icon.

3. Search for a simple demo query to use for this exercise. Find a query and open it. Click OK to complete the creation of the DataProvider. In this case we are leaving the default name of DP_1.

4. Click OK to return to the worksheet.

5. Click on the placeholder for the analysis grid in cell F11. We will assign the same DataProvider to this analysis grid item. Using the dropdown box for existing DataProviders, select DP_1. Click OK.

Now the workbook is all set. To look at the results of this custom template, switch from the current Design mode back to Analysis mode by clicking on the Design mode icon (the left-most icon on the BEx Design toolbar). The results of the query appear with the customized template as shown in Figure 3.13.

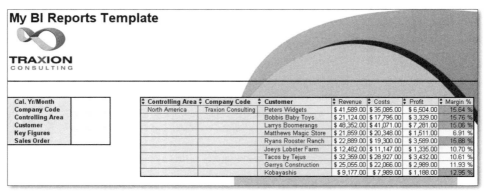

Cal. Yr/Month			
Company Code			
Controlling Area			
Customer			
Key Figures			
Sales Order			

Controlling Area	Company Code	Customer	Revenue	Costs	Profit	Margin %
North America	Traxion Consulting	Peters Widgets	$ 41,589.00	$ 35,085.00	$ 6,504.00	15.64 %
		Bobbis Baby Toys	$ 21,124.00	$ 17,795.00	$ 3,329.00	15.76 %
		Larrys Boomerangs	$ 48,352.00	$ 41,071.00	$ 7,281.00	15.06 %
		Matthews Magic Store	$ 21,859.00	$ 20,348.00	$ 1,511.00	6.91 %
		Ryans Rooster Ranch	$ 22,889.00	$ 19,300.00	$ 3,589.00	15.68 %
		Joeys Lobster Farm	$ 12,482.00	$ 11,147.00	$ 1,335.00	10.70 %
		Tacos by Tejus	$ 32,359.00	$ 28,927.00	$ 3,432.00	10.61 %
		Gerrys Construction	$ 25,055.00	$ 22,066.00	$ 2,989.00	11.93 %
		Kobayashis	$ 9,177.00	$ 7,989.00	$ 1,188.00	12.95 %

Figure 3.13 Custom Workbook Template with Embedded Query Results

It is possible to make this custom template the default for every query that is executed. Complete the following steps to assign a default template for all queries that are opened using the BEx Analyzer:

1. Open the workbook that will be used as the default.

2. Using the BEx Analysis toolbar, select the Global Settings icon.

3. Click on the Default Workbook tab. Select Use Current. Click OK. This workbook is now assigned as your default.

4. Close the current workbook.

Any new queries that are executed (for this particular user) will use the custom template. To undo this change, return to the Global Settings and select the Use SAP Standard button found under the Default Workbook tab. An administrator of the SAP BI system can also define different default custom templates to different users. This is done by making entries in the RSRWBTEMPLATE table.

3.5 Creating a Workbook with Multiple Reports

Creating custom templates and inserting a query allows you to dictate the look and feel of your reports to match current corporate standards, or to create new styles for individual business units.

Another key feature of workbooks is that they enable you to embed more than one query into a single worksheet. This feature is good for small queries with known dimensions

Inserting multiple queries into a single worksheet, or placing individual queries on separate worksheets, enables you to keep a series of reports within a single workbook.

The process of inserting an additional query is always the same, whether the intended destination is the same worksheet or a new one.

Try the following:

1. Open the BEx Analyzer and execute a query.

2. To insert an additional query, click on or insert a new worksheet. Switch to Design mode and place a new analysis grid at the desired location.

3. Click on the placeholder for the analysis grid and assign it to a new DataProvider that references a different query definition.

When exiting Design mode, the query results are embedded into this second worksheet.

3.6 Workbook Settings

When opening a workbook, a user can choose to have data automatically refreshed to ensure that the most current information is always displayed. If the last saved version of the workbook is to be saved then the autorefresh feature should be turned off. This setting is found through the Workbook Settings icon, which is the right-most icon found on the BEx Design toolbar. Workbook setting functions can also be used to apply themes to individual workbooks.

There are a series of tabs found in the Workbook Settings window. The General tab (shown in Figure 3.14) allows an individual user to set the following properties:

▶ Refresh Workbook on Open — If selected, a workbook is automatically refreshed with values from the BI server when opened. If not selected, a user must manually refresh the report to see the most current results.

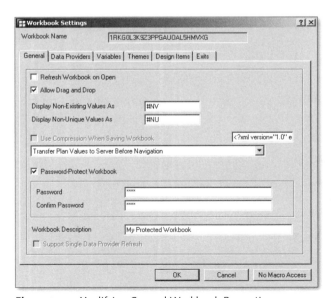

Figure 3.14 Modifying General Workbook Properties

▸ Allow Drag and Drop — This is the default behavior for workbook navigation, however, it can be turned off by unchecking the indicator box.

▸ Password-Protect Workbook — Activating password protection will allow a user to navigate using OLAP functions but will block any attempts to enter or modify data found in the analysis grid. If a user attempts to insert a new design item, the BEx Analyzer will request the password. If a user knows the password they can unlock this feature by following the menu path TOOLS • PROTECTION • UNPROTECT SHEET using the Excel menu.

▸ Workbook Description — The description for the workbook saved to the BI server can be changed using the text box found here.

BEx Themes can also be modified using the Workbook Settings function. BEx Themes consist of a set of Excel-style definitions that are used in the workbook. You can adjust a theme to modify background color, fonts, font styles, font sizes, etc. Themes are stored on the BI server and are based on Stylesheet classes. A user can create a custom theme by customizing Stylesheet classes and then saving a new BEx Theme using the Workbook Settings option. For example, a user wants to change the formatting associated with the Row headings found in a report. The current font is considered too small. The style should be modified to enlarge the font and to make it bold. The default theme is shown in Figure 3.15.

Table

Controlling Area	Company Code	Customer	Revenue	Costs	Profit	Margin %
North America	Traxion Consulting	Peters Widgets	$ 41,589.00	$ 35,085.00	$ 6,504.00	15.64 %
		Bobbis Baby Toys	$ 21,124.00	$ 17,795.00	$ 3,329.00	15.76 %
		Larrys Boomerangs	$ 48,352.00	$ 41,071.00	$ 7,281.00	15.06 %

Figure 3.15   The Default Style Depicted for Controlling Area, Company Code, and Customer

1. Highlight a cell that contains a row heading.

2. Follow the Excel menu path and choose FORMAT • STYLE

3. The style named SAPBEXchaText is displayed. Click the Modify button to change the preset style definition.

4. Change the font style to Bold and the font size to 11. Click OK.

To save this modification as part of the overall theme that BEx uses for this workbook, click on Workbook Settings and save a New theme under the Themes tab. To apply this custom theme to future workbooks a user must click on the Workbook Settings icon and:

1. Highlight the custom theme and click Apply.

2. Select the Reapply Theme Before Rendering button.

3. Click OK to finish the change.

The changes using the customized theme are reflected in Figure 3.16.

Table						
Controlling Area	**Company Code**	**Customer**	Revenue	Costs	Profit	Margin %
North America	Traxion Consulting	Peters Widgets	$ 41,589.00	$ 35,085.00	$ 6,504.00	15.64 %
		Bobbis Baby Toys	$ 21,124.00	$ 17,795.00	$ 3,329.00	15.76 %
		Larrys Boomerangs	$ 48,352.00	$ 41,071.00	$ 7,281.00	15.06 %
		Matthews Magic Store	$ 21,859.00	$ 20,348.00	$ 1,511.00	6.91 %

Figure 3.16 Customized Style Applied for SAPBEXchaText

3.7 Text Elements

Text elements provide housekeeping information about a query, such as the author of the query, when it was last changed, and the name of the InfoProvider that the query is based on. Text elements appear under the Information heading in the BEx standard workbook. In NetWeaver BI 7.0, the text elements are referred to as Constant Text Elements. The available constant text elements include:

► Created By

► Last Changed By

► InfoProvider

► Query Techincal Name

► Query Description

► Key Date

► Changed On

► Current User

► Last Refreshed

► Status of Data

Most of these elements are self-explanatory. Key Date and Status of Data require further definition. Key Date is the date used for which time-dependent master data (if applicable) is selected against. If a key date is not defined, then the system date is used automatically.

Master data for some characteristic InfoObjects is time dependent, meaning that it has a valid from and to date. The key date entered into the query will pick up the master data that has a date range that spans the key date.

Status of Data provides the date and time when data was last posted to the InfoProvider. In other words, it tells you exactly how recent the data in the InfoCube is. If an SAP BI system refreshes an InfoCube weekly, then data can be up to one week old before receiving the next update. If an SAP BI system updates an InfoCube on a nightly basis, the data results of a query are lagged by one day from the operational source system. For MultiCubes that are constructed from many InfoCubes, the date and time shown for Status of Data reflects the individual InfoCube with the oldest date and time.

The date and time displayed are shown in the local time zone for the actual BI server. A server in France may be 6 hours ahead of a user accessing a report in New York. Be aware of this when looking at dates and times in the Text Elements.

3.8   Working Offline

The BEx Analyzer provides an option to view data in the Results area without being connected to the BI server. It is possible to provide these offline results by modifying the Data Provider properties that are assigned to BEx Design items found in the workbook.

For example, an analysis grid that is sourcing data from a query definition can be configured to provide this information in an offline scenario.

To activate this function a user must switch to the BEx Analyzer Design mode. Once in Design mode, a user simply clicks on a Design item, which presents the Properties Dialog as shown in Figure 3.17. From this pop-up window a user can modify the Data Provider settings by clicking on the Change Data Provider icon. Check the Provide Results Offline to activate this option. This is typically done when working in Formula mode (discussed in the next section) to prevent formula errors when opening the workbook.

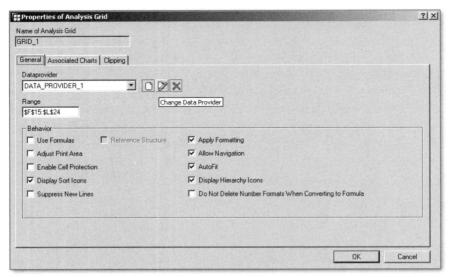

Figure 3.17 Properties of the Analysis Grid Design Item

3.9 Working in Formula Mode

When working in Formula mode, each cell in an analysis grid is replaced by a corresponding Microsoft Excel formula. By switching to Formula mode, a user can prevent standard BEx formatting from reappearing when refreshing results and navigating on a query.

The Convert to Formula function is used to switch to Formula mode. Convert to Formula can be found in the context menu when right-clicking on the analysis grid. This function will blow up the traditional link that BEx has between the actual design item and the results and instead retrieve information on a cell-by-cell basis using the Excel formulas found in each cell. Drag-and-drop functionality is deactivated once the Convert to Formula function is executed. Each value that remains in a cell definition contains a formula that starts with `BExGetData`. The number formatting provided by the query definition or navigation of a user also becomes deactivated by using Convert to Formula.

A recommended prerequisite for dividing a workbook into individual cell formulas is to configure the underlying Data Provider of the analysis grid to provider results offline. This is discussed in the preceding section of this chapter. This will avoid formula errors from being displayed when the workbook is opened at a later point in time.

Once Convert to Formula is applied, custom formatting can be accessed, and a new layout for a report can be constructed. Entire columns can be inserted into a worksheet that allow for additional calculations based off of the query key figures. In addition, BExGetData allows for standard Excel formatting, standard Excel formulas that can be wrapped around BExGetData, and the insertion of additional rows or columns. This allows a user to construct a presentation quality, highly formatted report that is no longer limited by the style restrictions of the standard BEx workbook. This typically works best when using a query definition that has a fixed matrix of predefined rows and columns, with no further drill downs possible. Leveraging this formula mode also allows users to create compound formulas that use the BExGetData formula as an operand. It is recommended that all subsequent formulas created by users follow syntax whereby the BExGetData component is found first in any formula string that is defined. A customized report that uses BExGetData and some custom Excel formulas is shown in Figure 3.18.

| E16 | ▼ | ƒx | =BExGetData("DATA_PROVIDER_1",E$12,$B16,$C16,$D16) | | | | | | |

A	B	C	D	E	F	G	H	I
	Controlling Area	**Customer**	**Company Code**	**Revenue**	**Top Revenue**	**Costs**	**Profit**	**Margin %**
	North America	Peters Widgets	Traxion Consulting	$ 41,589.00	$ 48,352.00	$ 35,085.00	$ 6,504.00	15.64%
	North America	Bobbis Baby Toys	Traxion Consulting	$ 21,124.00	$ 48,352.00	$ 17,795.00	$ 3,329.00	15.76%
	North America	Larrys Boomerangs	Traxion Consulting	$ 48,352.00	$ 48,352.00	$ 41,071.00	$ 7,281.00	15.06%
	North America	Matthews Magic Store	Traxion Consulting	$ 21,859.00	$ 48,352.00	$ 20,348.00	$ 1,511.00	6.91%
	North America	Ryans Rooster Ranch	Traxion Consulting	$ 22,889.00	$ 48,352.00	$ 19,300.00	$ 3,589.00	15.68%
	North America	Joeys Lobster Farm	Traxion Consulting	$ 12,482.00	$ 48,352.00	$ 11,147.00	$ 1,335.00	10.70%
	North America	Tacos by Tejus	Traxion Consulting	$ 32,359.00	$ 48,352.00	$ 28,927.00	$ 3,432.00	10.61%
	North America	Gerrys Construction	Traxion Consulting	$ 25,055.00	$ 48,352.00	$ 22,066.00	$ 2,989.00	11.93%
	North America	Kobayashis	Traxion Consulting	$ 9,177.00	$ 48,352.00	$ 7,989.00	$ 1,188.00	12.95%

Figure 3.18 Customized Report That Leverages Convert to Formula

3.10   Local Calculations

Local calculations allow a user to recalculate values and results based on specific criteria to that user. Local calculations only use the number found in the current view or navigational state of the report. They can only be created directly against the values displayed in the results, and cannot themselves, be used in subsequent calculations. Local calculations can be created by right-clicking on a Key Figure column in an analysis grid and choosing Properties. Selecting the Calculations tab provides a list of pre-defined functions (highlighted in Figure 3.19) that can be applied against single values for the key figure, or against any results rows that are turned on for a specific characteristic. In the case of single values the local calculation can also take on a cumulative effect whereby each individual value is added to the next, and so on. These local calculations are similar to the global calculations that can be assigned against a key figure definition using the BEx Query Designer tool. The available functions include:

- ▶ Average
- ▶ Average of nonzero values
- ▶ Counter
- ▶ Min/Max
- ▶ Rank
- ▶ Olympic Rank

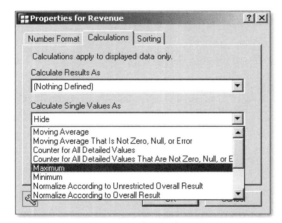

Figure 3.19 Creating Local Calculations Against a Key Figure

The Key Figures Properties dialog also allows a user to locally adjust the sort order of key figure values (in ascending or descending order), the scaling factors, and the number of decimal places.

3.11   Precalculating and Distributing Workbooks

Workbooks can be saved to either a local PC or to the SAP BI server. By using the Save function on the BEx Analyzer toolbar, you can:

- Save a new workbook
- Save as an existing workbook
- Save a query view
- Assign a workbook to a role

Saving a query view will save the current navigational state (view) of the data provider assigned to the Design item in the active cell. If the current view of the analysis grid is the source for a query view, a user must highlight a cell in this analysis grid. A saved query view can be used as a data provider for the BEx Web Application Designer (WAD), the BEx Report Designer, or the Visual Composer.

The save dialog allows a user to save new workbooks or query views to either favorites or roles. Both favorites and roles contain a folder tree structure for storing and managing content. Roles can be assigned to a user community whereas favorites are unique for each user. Think of roles as a publicly shared folder and favorites as a private folder for one user.

An alternative to saving workbooks to the BI server is to store them locally on a PC (see Section 3.8 to make sure the data is available offline). From the Microsoft Excel main menu, follow the path FILE • SAVE AS and provide a name for the workbook. One way to easily distribute a workbook in SAP BI, as seen in Figure 3.20, is to send it as an attachment via email using standard Microsoft Excel functionality. From the Excel menu path, select FILE • SEND TO • MAIL RECIPIENT (AS ATTACHMENT). The default mail client will open with a New Message window that has the subject populated and the BI workbook embedded as an attachment.

Figure 3.20 Distributing a Workbook Using Native Excel Functionality

The BEx Broadcaster can also be used to distribute and precalculate workbooks. The system generates a snapshot of the data and distributes the results at a specified time. The precalculated workbooks can be distributed via email or directly to the SAP Portal. The BEx Broadcaster can be launched using the Analysis toolbar within the BEx Analyzer. Choose the Tools icon and select Broadcaster. It is also possible to launch the BEx Broadcaster from other BEx tools and then select the appropriate workbook to broadcast. The BEx Broadcaster can be called from:

▶ BEx Query Designer

▶ BEx Report Designer

▶ BEx WAD

▶ BEx Analyzer Analysis toolbar (see Figure 3.21)

▶ An open session of the BEx Web Analyzer or BEx Web Application.

Configuring a broadcaster setting involves specifying the distribution type (email or portal) and the output format (Excel, Web Address, or URL). Additional settings allow larger objects to be sent as a compressed .ZIP file and with precalculation. A workbook that contains mandatory or optional user entry variables can have these variables assigned as part of the broadcaster setting. In the end, a broadcaster setting is saved with a technical name so that it can be located and modified later, if necessary. A broadcast setting for the workbook can be distributed at a specific time or only when changes are made to the underlying source data. Broadcast settings are scheduled after they have been saved.

> **Note**
>
> The Broadcaster option from the BEx Analyzer is only active when a workbook has been opened. If a query is executed in the BEx Analyzer, the Broadcaster is not available. After executing a query a user should save the embedded results as a workbook. This will open up access to the Broadcaster.

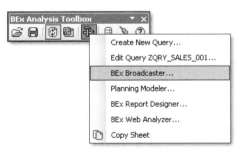

Figure 3.21 Launching the BEx Broadcaster from the Analyzer

The BEx Broadcaster launches in a web browser and presents a drop-down menu with different object types that can be broadcast. The Object Type should say

Workbook. Once the Object Type is defined, a workbook can be selected by clicking on the Open icon shown in Figure 3.22.

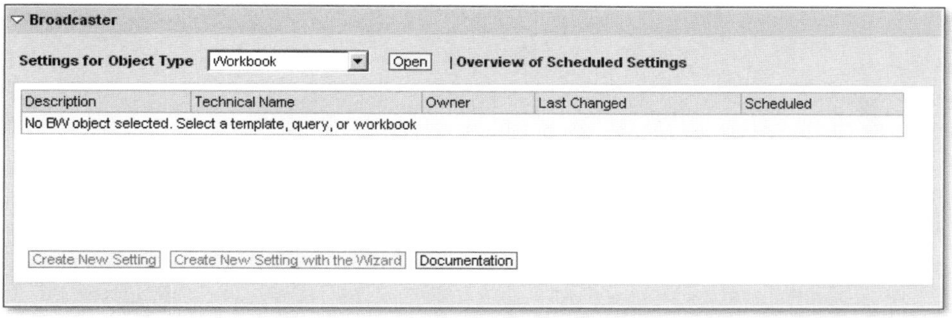

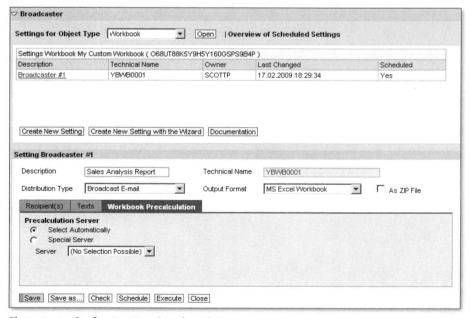

Figure 3.22 Creating Broadcaster Settings Against a Workbook

After choosing the Object Type (Workbook) and selecting a previously created workbook to use, the Broadcaster setting can be created by completing the following steps:

1. Select Create New Setting. A New Setting pane will appear similar to that shown in Figure 3.23.

Figure 3.23 Configuring New Broadcast Settings

> **Tip**
>
> Novice users may want to click on Create New Setting with the Wizard. This option provides a guided step-by-step path.

2. Enter a Description for the new setting.

3. Select a Distribution Type and an Output Format.

4. Select As ZIP File if sending larger workbooks.

5. Select the Texts tab and enter a subject heading and message to go along with the workbook (optional).

6. Select the Workbook Precalculation tab.

7. If the workbook contains variables they can be assigned here.

8. If a specific precalculation server is to be used it can be specified or the default setting of Select Automatically can be left as is.

9. Review the settings and then click on Save.

10. Provide a Technical Name for this setting. Click Transfer.

11. To distribute the workbook immediately, choose Execute.

12. To distribute the workbook in the future or on a recurring basis, choose Schedule and select the appropriate options.

Periodic scheduling of the broadcast setting can be done on a daily, weekly or monthly basis (see Figure 3.24), or as data is changed in the underlying InfoProvider.

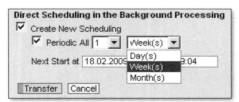

Figure 3.24 Periodic Scheduling of a Precalculated Workbook

3.12 Summary

The BEx Analyzer can be an excellent tool for presenting data and navigating reports. Using a Microsoft Excel environment leverages the existing knowledge of employees and facilitates their ability to access many well-known Excel features and functions. Changing the look and feel of reports through customized templates is an easy way of enhancing a reporting package with no required programming skills.

By utilizing standard SAP user security and authorization objects, information can be limited to only those who should see it. With the pervasiveness of email, it is virtually impossible to prevent data from spreading to unauthorized individuals; though that issue is best left for another discussion.

Printing reports in the BEx Analyzer has its limitations. A Microsoft Excel worksheet (using MS Excel 2003) cannot exceed 65,536 rows, and there is nothing that SAP BI can do to extend this. It can be argued that a meaningful report should never reach this dimension; however, it does happen on occasion. Issues regarding the width of a report come into play quite often when users attempt to print a snapshot of data. Adjusting the number of columns required in a report is one option, although it limits the usefulness of the query. Another alternative, and probably the best choice, is to train users to view and analyze data on-screen instead of on paper. While far from perfect, the BEx Analyzer is the primary reporting environment for SAP BI and it can be quite powerful when you know how to stretch its value.

4   Business Explorer (BEx) Web Reporting

BEx Web Reporting is a composite of all BEx tools that can be used to either create or display Web-based applications. It consists primarily of the BEx Web Analyzer and the BEx Web Application Designer (WAD). Additional user interfaces can also be developed using standard markup languages and the Web design Application Programming Interface (API), or by integrating a Visual Composer front-end.

4.1   BEx Web Analyzer

There are two primary tools for SAP Business Intelligence (BI) users to leverage via a web browser —the BEx Web Analyzer and the BEx WAD.

The BEx Web Analyzer has functionality similar to the BEx Analyzer that is integrated with Excel. The primary difference is that Web reports are viewed from a web browser and require no additional Graphical User Interface (GUI) software to use. Companies looking to save on desktop support costs may look at a purely Web-based rollout strategy.

More recent versions of SAP BI have dramatically improved the look and feel of Web reports. Creating a single query definition using the BEx Query Designer provides a user with the option of either displaying the results in a web page or in a BEx Analyzer workbook.

You can launch the standard Web reporting interface directly from the BEx Query Designer by simply clicking on the Execute icon in the BEx Query Designer toolbar. This is a very expedient way to create and test reports. When executed on the web, the output contains a navigation block and an analysis grid (see Figure 4.1).

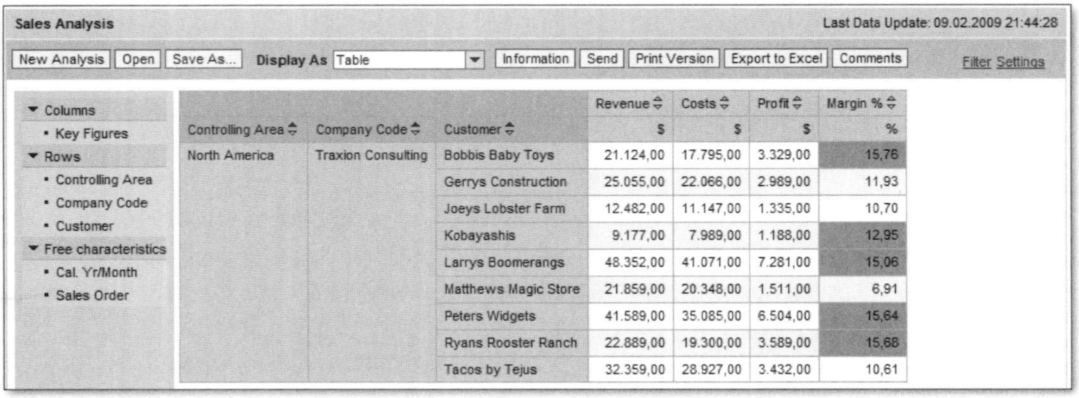

			Revenue ⇕	Costs ⇕	Profit ⇕	Margin % ⇕
Controlling Area ⇕	Company Code ⇕	Customer ⇕	$	$	$	%
North America	Traxion Consulting	Bobbis Baby Toys	21.124,00	17.795,00	3.329,00	15,76
		Gerrys Construction	25.055,00	22.066,00	2.989,00	11,93
		Joeys Lobster Farm	12.482,00	11.147,00	1.335,00	10,70
		Kobayashis	9.177,00	7.989,00	1.188,00	12,95
		Larrys Boomerangs	48.352,00	41.071,00	7.281,00	15,06
		Matthews Magic Store	21.859,00	20.348,00	1.511,00	6,91
		Peters Widgets	41.589,00	35.085,00	6.504,00	15,64
		Ryans Rooster Ranch	22.889,00	19.300,00	3.589,00	15,68
		Tacos by Tejus	32.359,00	28.927,00	3.432,00	10,61

Sales Analysis — Last Data Update: 09.02.2009 21:44:28

New Analysis | Open | Save As... | Display As Table ▼ | Information | Send | Print Version | Export to Excel | Comments | Filter Settings

Columns
• Key Figures
▼ Rows
• Controlling Area
• Company Code
• Customer
▼ Free characteristics
• Cal. Yr/Month
• Sales Order

Figure 4.1 Output of Query Definition Using a Web Browser

Interaction with the Web application varies depending on not only the Web item that is selected, but also on the context within an individual Web item (i.e., an analysis grid). A user can also use drag-and-drop functionality to update the content of the results by transferring characteristics between the navigation block and the analysis grid. Using the sample query illustrated throughout this book, a user can simply click and drag Sales Order from the Navigation Block to the results area. A guided proposal shows a user where a dragged object will be integrated into the results as it is directed over different elements of the analysis grid. This guided proposal is highlighted in Figure 4.2. Right-clicking on the analysis grid or the navigation block brings up an interactive Online Analytical Processing (OLAP) context menu.

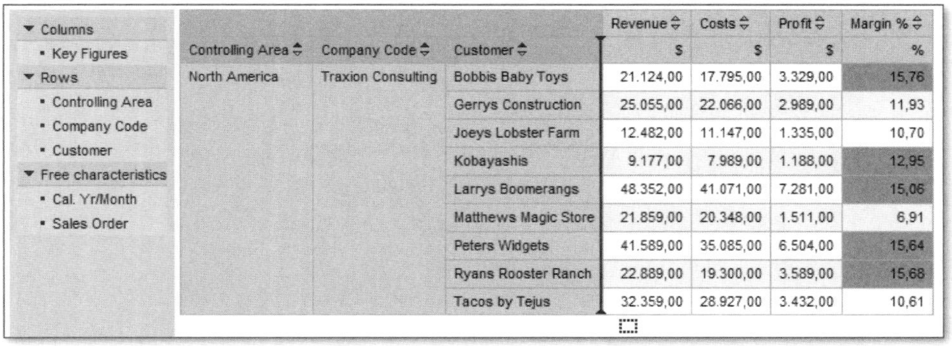

			Revenue ⇕	Costs ⇕	Profit ⇕	Margin % ⇕
Controlling Area ⇕	Company Code ⇕	Customer ⇕	$	$	$	%
North America	Traxion Consulting	Bobbis Baby Toys	21.124,00	17.795,00	3.329,00	15,76
		Gerrys Construction	25.055,00	22.066,00	2.989,00	11,93
		Joeys Lobster Farm	12.482,00	11.147,00	1.335,00	10,70
		Kobayashis	9.177,00	7.989,00	1.188,00	12,95
		Larrys Boomerangs	48.352,00	41.071,00	7.281,00	15,06
		Matthews Magic Store	21.859,00	20.348,00	1.511,00	6,91
		Peters Widgets	41.589,00	35.085,00	6.504,00	15,64
		Ryans Rooster Ranch	22.889,00	19.300,00	3.589,00	15,68
		Tacos by Tejus	32.359,00	28.927,00	3.432,00	10,61

Columns
• Key Figures
▼ Rows
• Controlling Area
• Company Code
• Customer
▼ Free characteristics
• Cal. Yr/Month
• Sales Order

Figure 4.2 Inserting a Characteristic via Drag and Drop

The BEx Web Analyzer serves as an ad hoc data analysis environment and is called by executing a query using the BEx Query Designer (typically by power users only) or via a Uniform Resource Locator (URL) or Portal iView. The standard Web Analyzer interface consists of numerous pushbuttons, a navigation block, and OLAP functions accessible via the context menu. The context menu is very similar to the BEx Analyzer (Excel) as it allows end users to access numerous functions such as drilldowns and filters, and also provides access to information broadcasting, printable reports, and the ability to save customized views of the data for usage at a later time. These query views are analogous to a customized BEx workbook. The pushbuttons available in the Web Analyzer header bar are shown in Figure 4.3.

Figure 4.3 Pushbutton Functionality Found in the BEx Web Analyzer

The available functions found in this header bar include:

- New Analysis
- Open
- Save As
- Display As
- Information
- Send
- Print Version
- Export to Excel
- Comments
- Filter (Web link — not a pushbutton)
- Settings (Web link — not a pushbutton)

The New Analysis button allows a user to open a data provider to perform ad hoc analysis with. The Open button lets a user retrieve analyses that have been completed previously and which are saved as query views to their favorites. The Save As button lets a user save custom views of the report currently being navigated on. A custom view of data can be saved to favorites or to the BEx Portfolio. The dropdown box allows data to be presented at a table, a chart, or as both at the same time. The default for the graphic type is a vertical bar chart. This is shown in Figure 4.4.

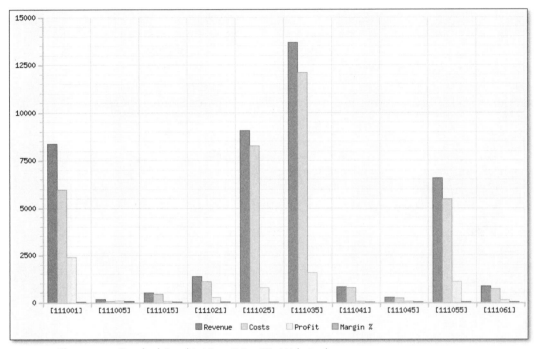

Figure 4.4 Standard Graphic View Using BEx Web Analyzer

The Information button provides general information about the underlying DataProvider being used in the query, and also lists any Static or Dynamic filters applied against the results and lists any variable values that were entered or calculated as part of the runtime execution. Static filters are the characteristic values that were selected in the query definition or from a user-entry variable at runtime. Dynamic filters are activated by a user and reflected by a change in navigational state from the original query. The general information includes the housekeeping facts that are referred to as text elements when using the BEx Analyzer. This information about the DataProvider includes the Query Technical Name, InfoProvider Technical Name, Query Created By, and the last data update (which shows how recent the data in the results is). The entire list of facts found in the Information window is shown in Figure 4.5.

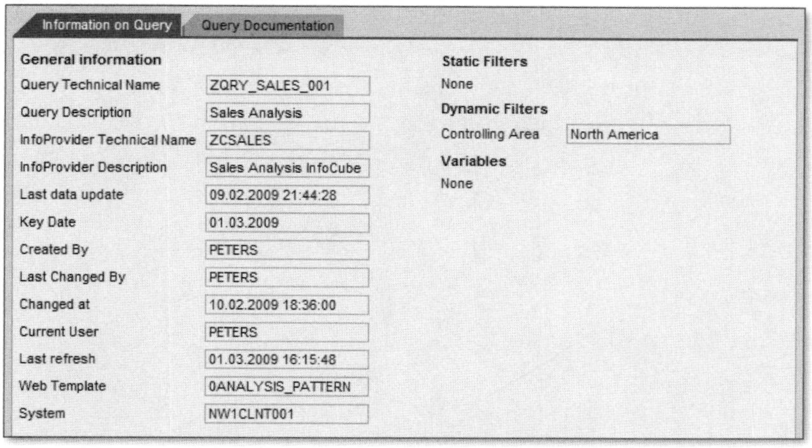

Figure 4.5 DataProvider Details Displayed from the Information Pushbutton

The Send button launches the information broadcasting wizard, which allows a user to configure the distribution and precalculation of query results and circulate them to a select group of users or email addresses. The Print Version button launches an Export dialog window, which presents options for adjusting headers, footers, margins, posterization, and page sizes (see Figure 4.6 for an example).

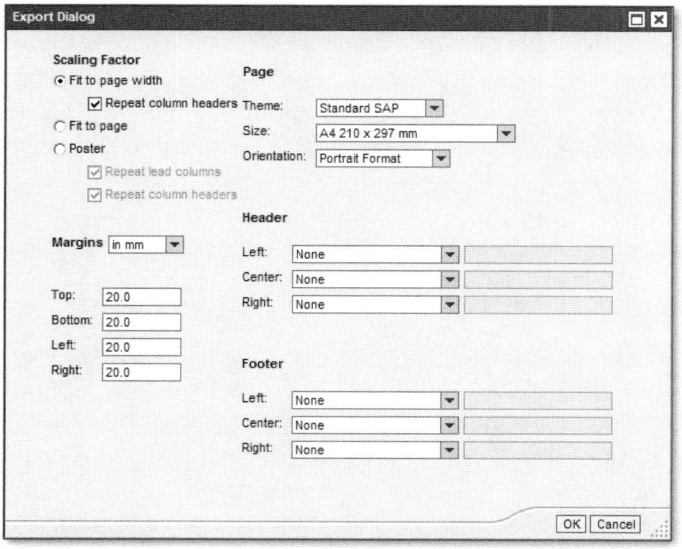

Figure 4.6 Print Options Available from the Print Version Button

After configuring the various print options, a user may click on the OK button, which results in the generation of a Portable Document Format (PDF) document. The PDF document contains the Web items found in the Web application and also lists any static/dynamic filters and variables used during the analysis. Not all Web items are able to be converted as part of a PDF document. The following Web items can be printed as a PDF:

▶ Analysis Grid

▶ Charts and Maps

▶ Info Fields (Text Elements)

▶ Conditions/Exceptions

▶ Free Text Fields

To leverage the Print Version options and export data as a PDF, the BI system administrator must properly configure the Adobe Document Services (ADS), which leverages the newer BI Java usage types. Larger reports will generally take more time to convert to a PDF. SAP states there is a technical limitation of 400 pages; however, this shouldn't be a factor as no individual analysis should require this much information to print. At a size this large, it would be better to rethink the usage of the information being consumed.

The Export to Excel button does just that. It exports the data displayed in the query to Microsoft Excel and embeds the results in a worksheet. Filters and Exception highlighting are also carried over to the Excel worksheet. Any graphics, such as a bar chart, become converted to a picture that gets exported, but as a flat image, does not allow for any downstream design changes. The Export function lets a user complete any necessary downstream calculations using Excel functions. The Comments button lets a user attach comments using a basic text input box or by using a formatted text toolbar similar to that found in word processing software. There is also a third option to upload documents that relate to the DataProvider.

In addition to these pushbuttons there are also two Web links that are found to the right of the row of pushbuttons. These links are labeled as Filter and Settings. The Filter link updates the Web report layout to include a Filter pane, which consists of a series of dropdown boxes — one for each characteristic and key figure structure that belongs to the DataProvider. If a variable screen is part of the query, this Filter pane provides access back to the variable values via a Variable Screen button. Selecting the Edit button from a characteristic dropdown box launches a Select

Values dialog that provides full-filter functionality to include/exclude value(s), to select individual value(s) or value range(s), and to locate specific values of interest using search functionality by either the Key or Text. The filter window is shown in Figure 4.7. Search settings can also be configured to display characteristic values that are:

1. found in the master data tables; or

2. posted to the dimension of the underlying InfoCube; or

3. only found in the current navigation state of the query.

These three options help manage the search volume for characteristics that have many unique values. Search settings are adjusted by clicking on the Settings icon found in the top right of the Select Values window.

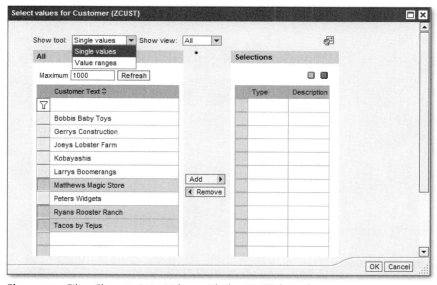

Figure 4.7   Filter Characteristics Values with the BEx Web Analyzer

The Settings link launches a Settings pane that provides numerous tabs to modify the properties of the overall query and the properties of the analysis grid (table) and graphic Web items. It also provides a tool for users to activate/deactivate global exceptions and conditions, or to define and create their own local exceptions and conditions against the local view of the query currently being analyzed. Descriptions of the tabs found via the Settings link are listed below.

- ▶ Table
  - ▶ Update the layout and visualization of the rows and cells found in the analysis grid
  - ▶ Display icons for context-specific documents that are attached to data, metadata, or master data.
  - ▶ Toggle on/off the display repeated texts and/or scaling factors
- ▶ Graphic
  - ▶ Change the default chart type (bar, area, pie, doughnut, etc.)
  - ▶ Set the location and type of chart legend
  - ▶ Insert Axis descriptions and labels
  - ▶ Swap the axes of the chart
- ▶ Exceptions
  - ▶ Toggle on/off global Exceptions
  - ▶ Create new local Exceptions using the Define Exception wizard
  - ▶ Define Exception wizard allows a user to set the Exception visualization to use background colors (default) or to display trend arrows with or without the cell value. See Figures 4.8 and 4.9 for examples. A Trend Exception type uses arrows as shown in Figure 4.9, while a Status Exception type uses traffic lights.

Exceptions displayed as	Legends for the table visualization		
	Distribution channel	Sales 2003	Sales 2004	Sales 2005
◉ Background color	Fax	$ 252,55	$ 172,74	$ 130,15
○ Symbol	Telephone	$ 130,18	$ 125,54	$ 129,71
○ Symbol and value	Internet	$ 58,32	$ 136,37	$ 22,64
○ Value and symbol				

Figure 4.8 Local Exception Defined with Background Color Visualization

Exceptions displayed as	Legends for the table visualization		
	Distribution channel	Sales 2003	Sales 2004	Sales 2005
○ Background color	Fax	↑ $ 252,55	$ 172,74	$ 130,15
○ Symbol	Telephone	→ $ 130,18	$ 125,54	$ 129,71
◉ Symbol and value	Internet	↓ $ 58,32	$ 136,37	$ 22,64
○ Value and symbol				

Figure 4.9 Local exception defined using Symbol and value visualization.

- Conditions
  - Similar to Exceptions, this tab allows a user to toggle on/off existing global Conditions or to create and define their own Conditions using a guided step-by-step wizard.
- DataProvider
  - Change the position and formatting of Results Rows
  - Set a size restriction for the number of cells retrieved in the results set
  - Change the display format of negative signs and zeros
  - Suppress zero values or entire rows/columns of zeros

4.2 BEx Web Analyzer Context Menu

Many features are available from the context menu. The context menu changes depending on the navigational state and the nature of the object that is selected when the context menu appears. A user can activate a context menu by right-clicking on any cell found in the analysis grid.

At the top of the context menu are the Back One Navigation Step and Back to Start menu options. Selecting Back One Navigation Step will undo the last navigational step that was performed on the query. Selecting Back to Start will return a user to the original navigational state of the query when it was first executed. Some other useful functions available from the context menu (shown in Figure 4.10) are:

- Goto
  - Navigate to any jump targets defined for the DataProvider using Report-Report-Interfacing (RRI). See Chapter 5 for more information.
- Filter
  - Keep Filter Value: Applies a filter on the selected characteristic value and removes the display of this information from the drilldown.
  - Keep Filter Value on Axis: Applies a filter on the selected characteristic value and keeps the display of this information in the drilldown.
  - Filter and Drilldown By: Applies a filter on the selected value and also adds a second characteristic to the drilldown.

▶ Select Filter Values: Allows multiple values to be selected as filter criteria.

▶ Remove Filter Value: Removes an applied filter.

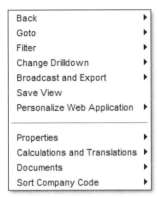

Back	▶
Goto	▶
Filter	▶
Change Drilldown	▶
Broadcast and Export	▶
Save View	
Personalize Web Application	▶
Properties	▶
Calculations and Translations	▶
Documents	▶
Sort Company Code	▶

Figure 4.10 Available Context Menu Functions

▶ Change Drilldown

   ▶ Drill Down By: Adds a characteristic to the drilldown and places this new information to the right of the position the function was called from.

   ▶ Swap <Characteristic> with: Replace the selected characteristic with another characteristic available in the free characteristics of the Filter pane.

   ▶ Remove Drilldown: Remove the selected characteristic from the results.

   ▶ Swap Axes: Swap the positions of the rows and the columns.

▶ Broadcast and Export

   ▶ Launch step-by-step settings for the Web application to be broadcast via email, the Portal, or a printer; or to export as a Comma Separated Value (CSV) file; or as a URL bookmark. When generating a bookmark, the URL will be found in the Web address bar on the web browser.

▶ Save View

   ▶ Creates a new reusable query view that can be accessed at a later point in time or used as a DataProvider in the WAD.

▶ Personalize Web Application

   ▶ After performing numerous ad hoc changes to a Web query, personalization will return a user to the navigational state that was set when personalization was saved. This allows a specific user to return to the actual layout of a query that they prefer. Once personalization has been turned on, it can be removed by selecting Delete Personalization under the same menu.

▶ Properties

   ▶ Apply various settings to characteristics, cells, or an axis in the analysis grid. These properties (such as Key/Text display) have been described in earlier chapters.

▶ Calculations and Translations

   ▶ Global Currency Translation: Making currency translations for currencies that are maintained in the system can be done using this menu. A user can select a specific currency to apply against the key figures and structure elements and have these values converted to the preferred currency.

   ▶ Right-clicking on a key figure heading brings additional options to perform calculations on the values using functions such as Min, Max, Moving Average, Rank, and Olympic Rank.

▶ Documents

   ▶ Works like the Comments pushbutton found in the Web Analyzer header bar. It provides functionality to add comments and formatted HTML text, or upload documents of any type and store them against the cell that was highlighted when the context menu was evoked.

▶ Sort <object>

   ▶ Can be applied against characteristics or key figures.

   ▶ Sorting a characteristic can be done in ascending or descending order on either the text description or the key of the characteristic values.

   ▶ Sorting numeric values of a key figure can be done in ascending or descending order.

The BEx Web Analyzer has many OLAP functions. You can usually access a single feature or function from more than one location (e.g., pushbutton, Web link, context menu). It really becomes a matter of user preference as to how a particular navigational change is carried out. The BEx Web Analyzer is a terrific tool for ad hoc analysis. It adds value by allowing users to store their own preferred navigational states as query views, bookmarks, or with personalization, and to reference them at a later time.

4.3 Overview of the WAD

The BEx WAD is a standalone application, accessed from the BEx menu path within a Windows Start menu. Typically, you open BEx WAD by navigating to START • PROGRAMS • BUSINESS EXPLORER • WEB APPLICATION DESIGNER (see Figure 4.11).

Launching the WAD prompts a user to log on to a specific SAP BI system. From the SAP Logon pad (shown in Figure 4.12), select the appropriate SAP BI environment. Click OK.

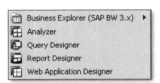

Figure 4.11 Accessing the WAD

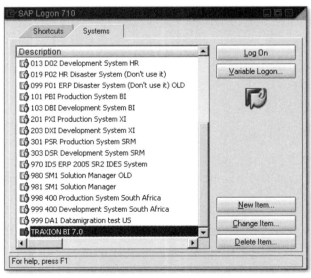

Figure 4.12 Selecting the Appropriate SAP BI Environment

118

The SAP BI system then prompts a user for valid logon credentials. A snapshot of the logon screen is shown in Figure 4.13. Enter the following information:

▶ Client (#)

▶ User (ID)

▶ Password

▶ Language (two-digit code. "EN"—English, "FR"—French)

Figure 4.13   Logging on to SAP BI to Access the BEx WAD

Once you have entered the required information, click OK. The BEx WAD is displayed in a new window (see Figure 4.14).

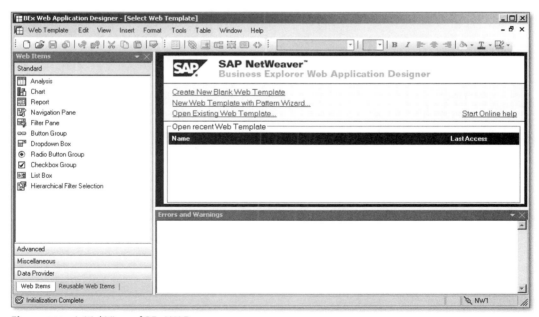

Figure 4.14   Initial View of BEx WAD

The WAD is a graphical standalone tool, which allows report designers to author and publish Web templates. Web templates are HTML pages that incorporate SAP Business Warehouse (BW) queries and query objects such as tables, graphics, and maps. These Web applications can be static or dynamic.

The WAD is similar to other web page publishing software, and no prior HTML knowledge is required to use it. SAP BI–specific placeholders are inserted on a page and these placeholders are dynamically replaced with the data from a query result at runtime. These Web applications combine regular web page content such as text, pictures, and links with additional content from a SAP BW system. BI-specific placeholders are referred to as Web items. The WAD provides many prebuilt Web items, such as analysis grids, charts, and dropdown boxes. There are also more advanced Web items, such as tab pages, maps, and input fields. In total, there are more than 30 prebuilt Web items that a developer can simply drag and drop into a new Web application. These BI Web items, along with the usual Web publishing functions, constitute an SAP BI Web template.

4.4 WAD Layout

The BEx WAD is a what-you-see-is-what-you-get (WYSIWYG) application; however, the templates can also include HTML and JavaScript. Adding HTML tags, JavaScript, Multipurpose Internet Mail Extensions (MIME) includes (.js, .css), URLs, and frames are all possible with some direct coding efforts. That being said, users can create complex templates with no coding required. In terms of vocabulary, a Web template is the document displayed in the WAD, and a Web application is the resulting page that gets displayed in a web browser. For simplicity, this book considers a Web template to be analogous to a Web application.

The WAD provides an HTML view that lists generated HTML code and allows direct manipulation of the code if required. When a Web template is saved, it is assigned a unique Web address, which is also referred to as a URL. This URL can be copied and sent to users, thereby allowing them direct access to a reporting application via a web browser. The BEx WAD consists of five distinct sections (identified in Figure 4.15):

1. BEx WAD toolbar/menubar

2. Web Items pane

3. Properties pane

4. Web Template pane

5. Errors and Warnings pane

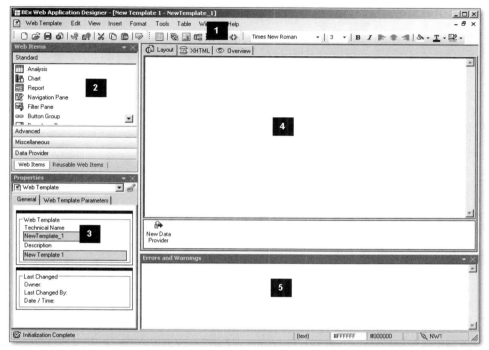

Figure 4.15 The Main Areas of the WAD

There are many functions accessible from both the menu paths and the toolbar icons. The key features found in the menu paths are summarized in the following list. Each item listed also corresponds to the individual icons displayed in Figure 4.16.

- ► Web Template (menu path)
  - ► New
  - ► Open
  - ► Save
  - ► Execute
  - ► Validate
  - ► Validate on Server

- ▶ Edit (menu path)
  - ▶ Cut
  - ▶ Copy
  - ▶ Paste
  - ▶ Correct and Format
- ▶ Insert (menu path)
  - ▶ Insert Table
  - ▶ Insert Hyperlink
  - ▶ Insert Image
  - ▶ Insert Language-dependent Text
  - ▶ Insert DIV tag
  - ▶ Insert SPAN tag
  - ▶ Insert any HTML tag
- ▶ Format (menu path)
  - ▶ Format Font
  - ▶ Format Font Size
  - ▶ Bold
  - ▶ Italic
  - ▶ Align Left/Center/Right
  - ▶ Background Color
  - ▶ Text Color
  - ▶ Text Background Color

Figure 4.16 BEx WAD Toolbar Icons

Most of the generic publishing functions found in the WAD work in the same way as using something like Microsoft Word. Cut, copy, paste, and inserting/formatting text are easily applied using these toolbar functions. Images can be added to a template by following the Insert menu path or by using the Insert Image icon.

To insert a picture, follow the menu path INSERT • IMAGE from the BEx WAD menu bar (see Figure 4.17). Images should first be placed in the Mime Repository in order for them to be used directly in a Web template.

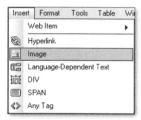

Figure 4.17 Adding an Image to a Web Template

The Web Items pane displays many predelivered objects that you can add to a web template document by simply using drag and drop functionality. Web items are inserted as placeholders into a web page where they are then configured to retrieve information from a specified DataProvider.

Standard Web items, displayed in Figure 4.18, such as tables and charts, are basic building blocks for Web applications. We templates can be made more interactive by adding dropdown boxes, radio buttons, and checkboxes. Note that you must link each Web item that you add to the template to an SAP BI DataProvider. Multiple Web items can reference a single DataProvider or each Web item can point to unique DataProviders.

Figure 4.18 Standard Web Items

Some of the more commonly used Web items are:

▶ Analysis Grid

  ▶ Data results are displayed in rows and columns with embedded OLAP functionality.

▶ Chart

  ▶ Graphical representations of data. Many standard chart types are available, including various bar charts, line diagrams, and pie charts.

▶ Dropdown Box

  ▶ Inserts a graphical dropdown box to display and select characteristic values to filter on.

▶ Navigation Pane

  ▶ Displays all characteristics and key figures and allows users to make navigational changes to the analysis grid. The context menu from a Navigation pane allows the ability to filter characteristic values and to add free characteristics to the analysis grid via drilldowns.

In addition to the Standard Web item grouping, there are also two other categories of Web items termed Advanced and Miscellaneous. The listing of Advanced and Miscellaneous web items is found in Figure 4.19 and Figure 4.20, respectively.

A somewhat unseen help feature provides further explanation on the nature of each Web item. By double-right-clicking on a Web item of interest, a small help area will appear that gives a short description about its usage. This is highlighted for the drop-down box Web item in Figure 4.21.

Figure 4.19 Advanced Web Items

Figure 4.20 Miscellaneous Web Items

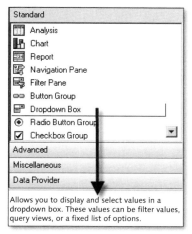

Figure 4.21 Help Area for Web Item Descriptions

The Properties pane consists of two tabs: General and Web Item/Template Parameters. The General tab, as displayed in Figure 4.22, displays the technical name and description at the Web template level, and shows the DataProvider assignment when a Web item is selected. All Web items have display parameters such as width, height, header, number of columns, etc., which can be adjusted to define the appearance and control the behavior within the application. The Web Item Parameters tab in the Properties pane lists all of the Display, Behavior, and Data Binding controls that can be adjusted. The individual parameters listed depend on the particular object selected. A dropdown box at the top of the Properties pane displays which object is currently being configured.

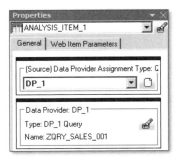

Figure 4.22 General Tab on the Properties Pane of the WAD

After inserting a Web item as a placeholder and making the required changes to the parameters, a well-defined customized Web item may be saved as a reusable Web item so that it can be leveraged again by other web template designers. Right-click on a Web item found in the Web template pane and select Save as Reusable Web Item. This will save the object to the SAP BI server and add it to the listing of Reusable Web Items tab, which is found at the bottom of the Web Items pane. Assigning a DataProvider to a Web item is done on the General tab of the Properties pane. All DataProviders assigned to a Web template are displayed in the center of the WAD tool, just below the Web template pane. This area is highlighted in Figure 4.23. New DataProviders can always be inserted by double-clicking on the New Data Provider icon.

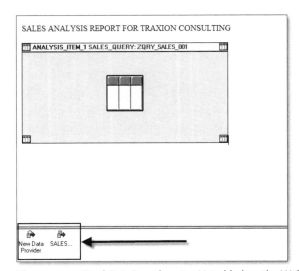

Figure 4.23 Used DataProviders Are Listed below the Web Template Pane

The Web Template pane, shown in Figure 4.24, displays the layout and an overall preview for how the Web application will look. Simply clicking in the Web Template pane allows a user to enter free text, and to leverage the toolbar icons to insert tables, images, and to format text properties. Dragging and dropping Web items from the Web Items pane to the Web Template pane will result in a BI placeholder that requires an assignment to a DataProvider. Web items can be resized as required by dragging on the handles of the placeholder outline.

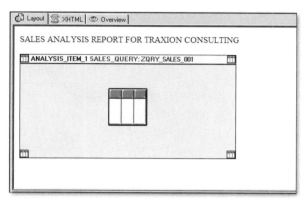

Figure 4.24   Web Template Pane Provides a Work Area for a Designer to Lay Out a New Web Application

There are three tabs associated with the Web Template pane and they can be seen in the top of Figure 4.24. These tabs are Layout, XHTML, and Overview. The Layout tab is selected by default and it serves as the work area for a designer to construct a new Web application. Underlying HTML code is generated each time an object is added to the work area of the Layout tab. This code is visible by clicking on the XHTML tab. The XHTML code can be directly modified or enhanced by a developer. It follows some color-coding conventions for different syntax elements (see Figure 4.25). A drop-down box at the top of this tab allows a user to place a pointer at different parts of the code by selecting a Web item name. Comments are colored in gray, HTML tags in black, and BI-specific content in dark red, for example. Any complex HTML editing can be done using an external program. The code found in a Web template can be exported to a file using the menu path WEB TEMPLATE • EXPORT TO FILE. When the code has been augmented it can be brought back into the WAD using the converse command path WEB TEMPLATE • IMPORT FROM FILE.

```
 SALES_QUERY                                                        ▾
<bi:bisp xmlns="http://www.w3.org/TR/REC-html40" xmlns:bi="http://xml.sap.com/2005/01/bi/wad/bisp" xmlns:jsp="http://java.sun.com/JSP/Page" >
  <html >
    <head >
      <title >BEx Web Application</title>
      <meta http-equiv="Content-Type" content="text/html; charset=utf-8" />
    </head>
    <body >
      <bi:QUERY_VIEW_DATA_PROVIDER name="SALES_QUERY" >
        <bi:INITIAL_STATE type="CHOICE" value="QUERY" >
          <bi:QUERY value="ZQRY_SALES_001" />
        </bi:INITIAL_STATE>
      </bi:QUERY_VIEW_DATA_PROVIDER>
      <p >SALES ANALYSIS REPORT FOR TRAXION CONSULTING</p>
      <p >
        <bi:ANALYSIS_ITEM name="ANALYSIS_ITEM_1" designwidth="405" designheight="200" webitem="BITM_20090302_215806" >
          <bi:DATA_PROVIDER_REF value="SALES_QUERY" />
        </bi:ANALYSIS_ITEM>
        <bi:TEMPLATE_PARAMETERS name="TEMPLATE_PARAMETERS" />
<!-- insert data providers, items and other template content here -->
      </p>
    </body>
  </html>
</bi:bisp>
```

Figure 4.25 XHTML View of the Web Template

The Overview tab (Figure 4.26) provides a summarized listing of all of the BI-specific objects, Web items, and commands that are included in the web template. It lists the Item Name and assigned DataProvider(s) in a table. Right-clicking on an entry lets a user rename the item or edit the parameters in a separate pop-up window.

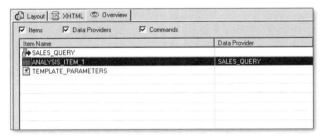

Figure 4.26 Overview Tab Lists BI Objects in a Summarized Table

The Errors and Warnings pane found at the bottom of the WAD is used to present any errors or warning messages that exist in the current state of a Web template. Every couple of seconds a local validation is performed on the Web template structure. This default of two seconds is a property that can be adjusted by following the menu path TOOLS • SETTINGS. A manual validation can also be performed against the server by clicking on the Validate icon found in the main toolbar. This check can also be triggered via the menu path WEB TEMPLATE • VALIDATE ON SERVER. The Errors and Warnings pane can also be relevant when a developer edits code directly in the XHTML view. To check for errors or warnings after editing the code, follow the menu path EDIT • CORRECT AND FORMAT. This command will readjust the color coding of the elements and identify any syntax errors.

Navigating the different panes and tabs found within the WAD is easy once a user has some familiarity with the tool. There are also keyboard shortcuts that take a user directly to a particular area. Some shortcuts include:

- ▶ `Ctrl`+`Shift`+`W` — Web Items
- ▶ `Ctrl`+`Shift`+`P` — Properties
- ▶ `Ctrl`+`Shift`+`R` — Reusable Web Items
- ▶ `Ctrl`+`Shift`+`E` — Errors and Warnings
- ▶ `Ctrl`+`Shift`+`S` — Status Bar
- ▶ `Ctrl`+`Shift`+`L` — Layout Tab
- ▶ `Ctrl`+`Shift`+`X` — XHTML Tab
- ▶ `Ctrl`+`Shift`+`O` — Overview Tab

4.5   Creating a Web Template

The minimum prerequisite for creating a Web template is having a source query definition or a query view (saved from a primary query definition) available for use. If a query definition needs to be created, the BEx Query Designer can be called directly from the BEx WAD. Queries that are referenced as DataProviders can be viewed and updated while constructing a Web template. To launch the BEx Query Designer from the BEx WAD menu path, choose TOOLS • QUERY DESIGNER.

4.5.1   Creating a Web Template

Launch the WAD and use the following process to create a basic design of a typical Web application.

1. Click on Create New Blank Web Template.
2. Enter a title for the Web application. Click in the Layout area to place the active cursor. Enter a descriptive title, such as Sales Analysis Reporting and hit `Enter`. Highlight the inserted text and select a Font, Font Size, and Font attributes using the WAD toolbar.

3. Select an analysis grid (called Analysis) from the Standard Web Items tab (see Figure 4.27) and drag it to the Layout window below the title.

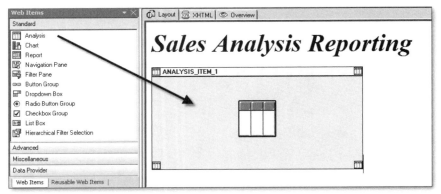

Figure 4.27   Step 3: Inserting an Analysis Grid Web Item

4. Select a Query/Query View to provide data for the new analysis grid item. Figure 4.28 shows the assignment of a Query/View.

In the Properties pane, ensure that ANALYSIS_ITEM_1 is selected and then click on the New Data Provider icon (it looks like a blank page). In the Name field, enter SALES_QUERY (spaces are not allowed). Next, select Query or Query View for the Data Provider Type and use the corresponding button to locate and assign the correct DataProvider. The name of a DataProvider can be changed later on, if necessary. Try to provide a clear description of each DataProvider to avoid confusion as the complexity of a Web application will likely increase as more objects are added.

Figure 4.28   Step 4: Selecting a Query/Query View to Provide Data

5. Define the parameters and attributes (shown in Figure 4.29) for the Analysis Web item. Click on the Web Item Parameters tab under Properties. Context-specific help is displayed in the bottom of the Properties pane for each of the properties listed. For an analysis grid it's important that you set the Number of Data Rows Displayed at Once to something manageable. The most relevant parameters to focus on from a reporting perspective are found under the sub-headings Display, Internal Display and Paging.

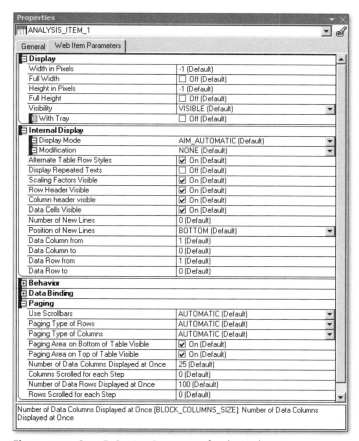

Figure 4.29   Step 5: Setting Parameters for the Web Item

6. Add additional Web items, such as Chart, to the Web template by repeating Steps 3 through 5.

7. When finished, click the Validate icon found in the WAD toolbar to ensure there are no errors or missing assignments.

8. If interested, click the XHTML tab to view the generated code for the constructed Web application (optional).

9. Save the Web template. Click on the Save icon found in the WAD toolbar or use the keyboard shortcut $\boxed{\text{Ctrl}}$+$\boxed{\text{S}}$. Provide a description and a technical name for this new Web application.

10. The Web template can now be executed by simply clicking on the Execute icon found in the WAD toolbar. A screenshot for a similar Web application is displayed in Figure 4.30.

Sales Analysis Reporting

Controlling Area ⇕	Company Code ⇕	Customer ⇕	Revenue ⇕	Costs ⇕	Profit ⇕	Margin % ⇕
			$	$	$	%
North America	Traxion Consulting	Bobbis Baby Toys	21.124,00	17.795,00	3.329,00	15,76
		Gerrys Construction	25.055,00	22.066,00	2.989,00	11,93
		Joeys Lobster Farm	12.482,00	11.147,00	1.335,00	10,70
		Kobayashis	9.177,00	7.989,00	1.188,00	12,95
		Larrys Boomerangs	48.352,00	41.071,00	7.281,00	15,06
		Matthews Magic Store	21.859,00	20.348,00	1.511,00	6,91
		Peters Widgets	41.589,00	35.085,00	6.504,00	15,64
		Ryans Rooster Ranch	22.889,00	19.300,00	3.589,00	15,68
		Tacos by Tejus	32.359,00	28.927,00	3.432,00	10,61

Figure 4.30 Executing a Web Application with Internet Explorer

The BEx WAD generates a URL that can be shared with other users so they can access the saved Web template. This URL can be copied and pasted into the body of an email to share with others. It can then be saved as a web page bookmark using Internet Explorer (IE).

Tip

Microsoft IE refers to bookmarks as Favorites. When viewing a Web template with IE, simply follow the path FAVORITES • ADD TO FAVORITES. This stored Favorite can be recalled at a later time.

To generate the URL for a Web template, follow the WAD menu path WEB TEMPLATE • PUBLISH • COPY URL INTO CLIPBOARD.

An easy way for new developers to learn how to create Web applications with various web items is to leverage the Pattern Wizard, which provides shell templates that have a preconfigured assortment of web items, layouts, and data providers. After launching the WAD, choose the option New Web Template with Pattern Wizard from the list of links displayed. For example, a preexisting Web template that contains an analysis grid, chart, and two different DataProviders can be leveraged by selecting Small Web Template with Chart, Analysis Web Item, and 2 DPs. The WAD then leads a developer through various steps (see Figure 4.31) that determine the overall layout, title, and DataProvider assignments. This approach quickly expedites the creation of simple Web templates and helps a developer learn how to use the tool with some assistance. As a developer becomes more proficient they can then choose to customize the actual WAD patterns to meet their needs.

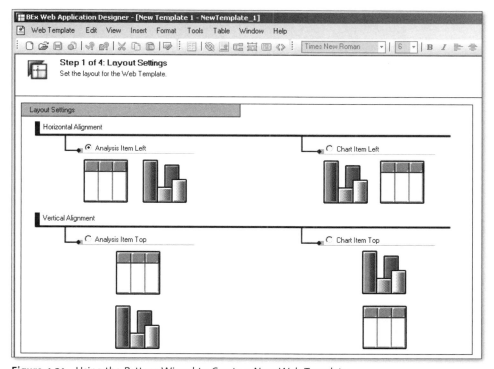

Figure 4.31 Using the Pattern Wizard to Create a New Web Template

4.6 Inserting Additional DataProviders

If a single DataProvider has already been assigned to a Web template, dragging a Web item onto the Layout area creates a placeholder for that item and assigns it to the previously defined DataProvider. Data is brought into a Web application via the following steps:

1. A query definition is created with the BEx Query Designer.

2. A Web item is inserted into a Web template using the WAD.

3. A Web item is assigned to a DataProvider.

4. A DataProvider represents a query definition or query view.

Adding subsequent web items to the template will also result in the same DataProvider being assigned. This is ideal if the web application consists of different graphical representations (table, chart) and navigational options (dropdown box, generic navigational block). One of the real strengths of using the BEx WAD is the ability to reference data from more than one query or query view. Combining data from numerous InfoProviders or DataProviders on one screen is extremely powerful. It allows different types of functional information to be presented seamlessly to the user.

To add DataProviders, click on the New Data Provider icon located at the bottom of the Layout area.

The following is a summary of the steps that result in a new DataProvider being created (shown as DATAPROVIDER_2 in Figure 4.32):

1. Insert a Web item into the Web template.

2. Ensure that you have selected the Web item.

3. Select the General tab in the Properties pane.

4. Click on the New DataProvider button.

5. Enter a unique name for the new DataProvider or leave the default.

6. Assign a query or query view to the new DataProvider.

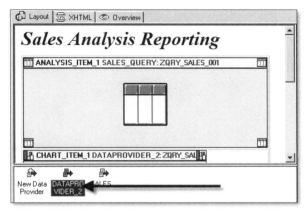

Figure 4.32   Multiple DataProviders Created within a Single Web Application

4.7   Inserting Tables

When many Web items are added to a Web template, it may be helpful to structure them within a table. The WAD provides basic table functionality, including the ability to insert and delete extra rows, cells, and columns. Use the Insert Table icon in the WAD toolbar and enter an appropriate number of rows and columns using the sliders (see Figure 4.33) or the text entry boxes.

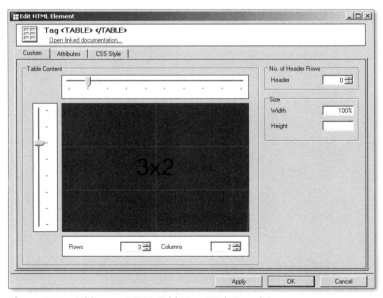

Figure 4.33   Adding an HTML Table to a Web Template

Basic attributes such as cell padding and cell spacing can also be defined. Figure 4.34 shows Web items contained within a 2 x 2 table. Further customization is done by simply switching to the XHTML view.

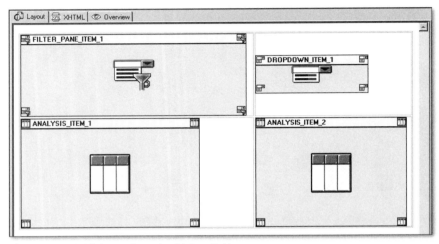

Figure 4.34 Web Items Organized into a Table

Another nice feature of the WAD is that it enables you to assign more than one DataProvider to a single navigational Web item. This simplifies navigation and greatly adds to the usability of Web applications. For example, picture a Web template consisting of two tables, each with its own unique DataProviders and source queries:

▶ Table A contains a Cost Center report for salaries.

▶ Table B contains a Cost Center report for travel and expenses.

Both queries contain the Cost Center characteristic. A user looking at the Web application may want to filter both of these reports to only show data for his Cost Center. This can be accomplished by using a dropdown box that filters both tables (i.e., both underlying DataProviders) simultaneously.

A dropdown box can affect one or more DataProviders. This is defined by a property of the Web item found in the Properties pane. Assuming the same Cost Center scenario, the following steps describe how to reference multiple DataProviders:

▶ Add a dropdown box to the Web template.

▶ Ensure that the dropdown box is selected.

- ▶ Click on the Web Item Parameters tab in the Properties pane.

- ▶ Expand the Data Binding options.

- ▶ Click on the grey Char/Structure button below the dropdown box.

- ▶ In the Edit Parameter pop-up window, locate 1 Affected Data Providers and choose the first DataProvider using the dropdown box.

- ▶ Click on the small green icon (shown in Figure 4.35) to insert a second DataProvider that will be controlled by this dropdown box Web item.

- ▶ Locate 2 Affected Data Providers and choose the second DataProvider using the dropdown box.

- ▶ Click OK to finish the Data Binding.

	Affected Data Providers	SALES_QUERY
	Affected Data Providers	DATAPROVIDER_2
	Affected Data Providers	Default
	Additional Action	INSTRUCTION_WITH_DEFAULT (Defaul
	Command via Command Wizard	
	Execution Point of Time	BEFORE (Default)
	Command	Default

Figure 4.35 Binding Multiple DataProviders to a Web Item

- ▶ Click on the Execute in the Browser icon in the BEx WAD toolbar to save and execute the Web application.

- ▶ Filtering an entry found for the characteristic assigned to the dropdown box Web item will update results for both SALES_QUERY and DATAPROVIDER_2.

4.8   Publishing Web Templates

Creating Web templates and testing them can be time-consuming. However, fine-tuning the format of the layout can greatly enhance the presentation of your Web application, which can benefit the usability for many users.

A couple of different distribution options are available to a report developer. Each template created with the BEx WAD is assigned its own unique URL. To find this URL, go to the BEx WAD toolbar and follow the path WEB TEMPLATE • PUBLISH • COPY URL INTO CLIPBOARD. You can then insert this URL into a document and send it to target users. More formally, Web applications can be published to either of the following:

▶ Role

▶ Enterprise Portal

▶ BEx Broadcaster

Each of these options is listed in the web template • publish menu of the BEx WAD toolbar. Publishing to a standard SAP BI Role is straightforward. A pop-up window (see Figure 4.36) lists all of the Roles that a report developer has access to publish to. Subfolders under each role can be created to organize content. The destination Role/folder is highlighted and the Web application is saved to that location.

A similar process is used to publish a Web template as a Portal iView in the Portal Content Directory (PCD). If you publish a Web template to the PCD, it is available as a BEx Web Application iView in the PCD. The system will automatically assign a technical name and propose a description for the web template, which can be renamed if desired. Following the menu path WEB TEMPLATE • PUBLISH • TO PORTAL will result in a pop-up dialog within the PCD. Navigate through the folder structure to find the appropriate destination for the iView. A Portal administrator can then use this new iView in an existing Portal role or page. The iView containing this Web template will be available to any user who has access to the assigned Portal role.

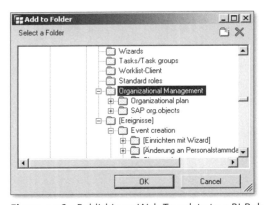

Figure 4.36 Publishing a Web Template to a BI Role

Publishing to the BEx Broadcaster provides distribution and precalculation options for the Web template. The BEx Broadcaster, discussed earlier, allows settings to be assigned in a step-by-step process that results in the Web template being broadcasted to by email, to a Portal, or to a printer. The parameters defined in these steps are saved as a setting for the individual Web application and can be cancelled or modified at a later time.

4.9   Summary

The WAD is an excellent development tool that allows for the creation of basic Web applications and highly complex dashboards using a WYSIWYG interface. These Web applications can source data from one or more Data Sources that can be seamlessly combined onto a single web page. The ability to make these link-ages with not only tabular displays, but also graphical representations, results in a richer user experience. Drag-and-drop functionality allows novice users to quickly build and deploy Web applications, while the XHTML view lets expert developers extend the capabilities of their Web applications. In future releases the WAD will be merged with the Business Objects' DashboardBuilder and Xcelsius and result in a new flagship dashboarding product for SAP BI users that has been referred to as Xcelsius+. In the meantime, the WAD is a stable product that has the capability to satisfy many reporting requirements for companies who deploy SAP Web reporting.

.

5 Report-to-Report Interface (RRI)

The RRI is a tool that enables users to link reports. RRI enables users to jump from one report to another that contains additional information. Maintaining this sender/receiver assignment is accomplished by creating a link within the SAP Business Intelligence (BI) system using Transaction code RSBBS. The receiver can be within or outside of the SAP BI system. Some of the receiver options are presented in Figure 5.1.

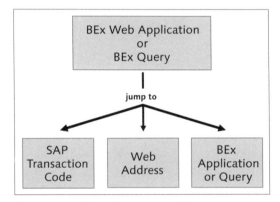

Figure 5.1 Linking Objects Using RRI

5.1 Overview

The RRI functionality can be used to predefine a preferred analysis path that takes a user from a summary level report all of the way down to the detailed document level; for example, enabling users to drill down to identify causes of variances. This also helps prevent performance issues that can result when large reports with a lot of data are executed. Breaking the business analysis down into smaller, modular chunks allows users to focus on variances and identify discrepancies, and thereby optimizes performance so you can be in a better position to generate high-quality reports.

RRI requires a minimum of two query definitions to jump from one report to another. The starting report is called the Sender and the destination report is called the Receiver.

These jump targets are defined for the Sender and are made available in the Online Analytical Processing (OLAP) context menu of a report. Figure 5.2 shows the Goto menu option in the context menu.

Figure 5.2 Accessing Jump Targets from the Goto Menu Option

5.2   Defining Jump Targets

You define a jump target by logging on to the SAP BI system via the SAP logon pad and executing Transaction code RSBBS. You can also follow the menu path Business Explorer • Query Jump Targets to define a jump target. The initial transaction screen is shown in Figure 5.3.

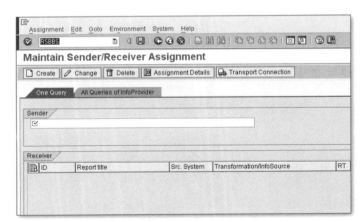

Figure 5.3 Maintain Sender/Receiver Assignment Screen

A Sender object can jump to a number of different report types, not just other SAP BI queries. Object types that can be assigned as Receivers include:

- Business Explorer (BEx) queries
- BEx Web applications
- BW 3.x Web applications
- BW Crystal Reports
- InfoSet queries
- Transaction codes
- ABAP reports
- Web addresses

Usually, sender/receiver assignments are made against BEx queries. Therefore, you should consider linking to an internal website that explains the data displayed in a query and provides supporting documentation and contact information for the business owner of a report.

The first step in creating a jump target is to choose the source query definition (the sender). Select the One Query tab in the Maintain Sender/Receiver Assignment screen. Enter the technical name of the query in the Sender field, or use the dropdown box to search by History, InfoAreas, Roles, or Favorites. The search functionality accepts partial text strings.

Figure 5.4 shows the query that has been assigned as the sender. Note that in Figure 5.4 the syntax for the sender is displayed as InfoProvider/technical query name.

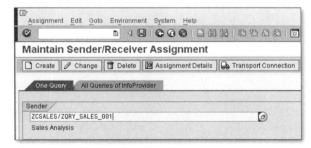

Figure 5.4 Selecting a Sender Query

You can maintain multiple sender/receiver assignments for a single query definition. This allows one report to serve as a jumping point to many other reports. To create a receiver, click on the Create button in the transaction toolbar. A pop-up window will prompt you to select a receiver in the Report Type section. Select the corresponding radio button. The receiver report type can point to the local SAP BI system or to another SAP system (i.e., an Enterprise Resource Planning (ERP) instance). Choose a target system (displayed in Figure 5.5)—either Local, if jumping to a transaction within the BI system, or Source System, if jumping to a transaction in another SAP system.

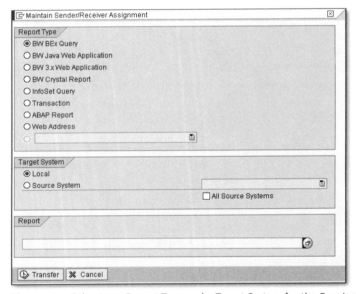

Figure 5.5 Selecting a Report Type and a Target System for the Receiver

Next, you must provide specific destination parameters for the receiver. The information to be populated will depend on the report type and target system that was selected earlier. Click the dropdown box in the Report Type section of the Maintain Sender/Receiver Assignment screen.

For a BW BEx Query report type, the resulting pop-up window (see Figure 5.6) will list all available query definitions. Highlight the appropriate query definition and click Open.

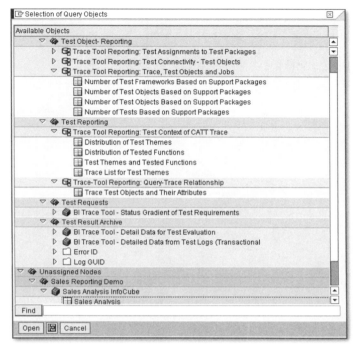

Figure 5.6 Selecting a Query Object as a Receiver

A Web application is selected in the same fashion. A pop-up window displays all of the available Web applications that can be selected as the receiver object.

If Transaction was selected as the receiver report type, the report developer can enter Transaction code RSRT directly into the Report text box. Pressing Enter transfers this assignment to the Report Type section and RSRT would appear with the selected receiver report type, Transaction, as seen in Figure 5.7.

If selecting a Web Address, clicking on the Report drop-down box at the bottom of the window results in a second pop-up window that allows you to enter text. Simply enter a full Web address in the format *http://www.traxionconsulting.com*

When the required information for the receiver has been entered, click on Transfer to return to the Maintain Sender/Receiver Assignment screen. This completes the sender/receiver link. All assignments against the selected sender are listed in a table in the Receiver section, as depicted in Figure 5.8.

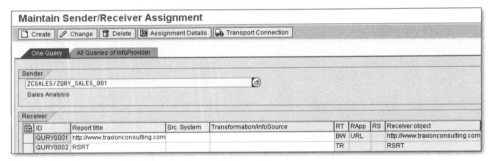

Figure 5.7 SAP Transaction Code RSRT as a Receiver

ID	Report title	Src. System	Transformation/InfoSource	RT	RApp	RS	Receiver object
QURY0001	http://www.traxionconsulting.com			BW	URL		http://www.traxionconsulting.com
QURY0002	RSRT			TR			RSRT

Figure 5.8 Summary of Existing Assignments for a Query

To change or delete an existing receiver assignment, highlight it and click on the corresponding button in the transaction toolbar. The Receiver table enables a report developer to edit the Report title for each Receiver object. The Report title is the text, which gets displayed in the Goto menu of the Sender Query.

This report title is the only description that an end user will see to inform them where each Goto entry will go, i.e., where users jump to next when they click on an element listed under the Goto menu. To change the Report title, simply highlight the existing text and replace it. The Receiver object references the specific destination.

This helps the report developer keep track of existing jump targets. The completed jump target assignments are shown in a BEx Web Report in Figure 5.9.

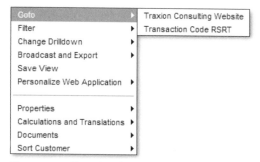

Figure 5.9 Completed Jump Target Assignments as Displayed in a BEx Web Report

For query-to-query definitions, the sender query serves as a filter by passing the contextual values of characteristics to a receiver query. The data that gets passed depends on where the Goto command was executed. For example, right-clicking on a Cost Center value of 1234 in the sender query and choosing the path GOTO • COST CENTER DETAIL REPORT will pass this single Cost Center as a parameter to the Receiver report. All data reflected in the Receiver report will only pertain to the preselected Cost Center 1234.

5.3   Summary

The collective capabilities provided by RRI and the BEx suite of tools (BEx Analyzer, BEx Web Reporting, and BEx Web Application Designer [WAD]) enable users to design, develop, and publish a wide range of reports and analytical applications.

Each of these tools requires sufficient time to learn and master, and more importantly, enough familiarity and creativity to exploit. Based on the underlying functionality in each tool, it is recommended that a new user spend some time with each tool and learn them in the following order:

1. BEx Query Designer
2. BEx Analyzer
3. BEx Web Reporting

4. BEx WAD

5. RRI

6. BEx Broadcaster

7. BEx Report Designer

8. Web Application programming Interface (API) and Visual Basic Applications (VBA) for Excel

By learning the tools in this order, users will understand the limitations and benefits of each application. Fortunately, with a Data Warehouse (DW), there is very little, if any, risk in allowing a new SAP BI report developer to experiment with the full suite of tools available to them. Therefore, it is recommended that users be given access to all of the tools, with the only limitation being the roles and locations that they can publish to. Periodic cleanup of unused test queries in a development or production environment is a minor trade-off for enabling users to become highly proficient with building queries, workbooks, and Web applications.

By thinking outside the box, and knowing how to stretch the functionality of the BEx tools, you'll discover solutions to satisfy your own unique reporting requirements. Having highly skilled report developers is fundamental to a successful deployment, which in turn raises overall adoption and Return on Investment (ROI) for the project owners.

6   Advanced Reporting Topics

To use custom images in a Web template, the images must first be stored in the MIME repository on the SAP Business Intelligence (BI) server. All MIME objects, such as graphics and icons, are saved as objects in the SAP database and can be referenced in Web reporting applications.

6.1   Storing Images in the Multipurpose Internet Mail Extensions (MIME) Repository

The MIME repository (shown in Figure 6.1) is accessed by logging into the SAP system with the logon pad and executing Transaction code SE80. The MIME repository is listed in the Object Navigator as part of the ABAP development workbench.

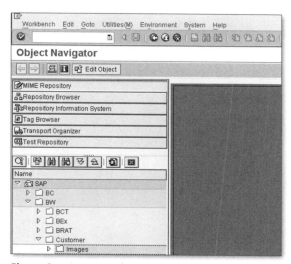

Figure 6.1   Accessing the MIME Repository via Transaction Code SE80

Graphic objects that are to be used in Web applications should be saved in the Business Warehouse (BW) folder. BW is the legacy name for SAP BI. It is recommended that a developer create subfolders under the menu path BW • CUSTOMER

• IMAGES. To create additional folders, simply right-click on an existing folder and choose CREATE • FOLDER. Once the desired location has been located, right-click on the folder of choice and choose Import MIME Objects. Saving graphics in the BW folder allows the objects to appear in the Business Explorer (BEx) Web Application Designer (WAD). Graphics or icons that are saved to the MIME repository are available to all users who have access to the BEx WAD. To insert an image from the MIME repository into a web template, choose INSERT • IMAGE (see Figure 6.2) using the WAD menu path. In the Edit HTML Element pop-up window, click on the source button (highlighted in Figure 6.2) to list the available images to select from. Numerous HTML attributes can be assigned to the image by clicking on the Attributes tab. Clicking OK will finish the process and insert the image into the Web template.

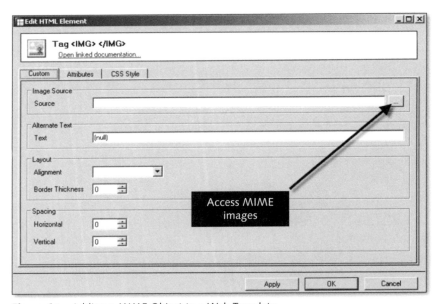

Figure 6.2 Adding a MIME Object to a Web Template

6.2 Personalization

Personalization is a function that, when activated, allows users to fill variable screens with specific values that can be saved and accessed later, and to also save user-specific layouts of reports that they prefer. Personalization data is stored by user ID and is found in table RSWR_PERS.

> **Note**
>
> Personalization must first be activated in order for it to be available for users. Once Personalization is turned on it cannot be deactivated.

Perform the following three setups to validate that personalization has been activated in your SAP NetWeaver BI system.

▸ Enter the Implementation Guide (IMG) (Transaction SPRO) and follow the menu path SAP NETWEAVER • BUSINESS INTELLIGENCE • SETTINGS FOR REPORTING AND ANALYSIS • GENERAL SETTINGS FOR REPORTING AND ANALYSIS • ACTIVATE PERSONALIZATION IN BEX.

▸ Check the status of the personalization settings. Three settings (Activate BEx History, Variables Personalization, and Web Report Person) are listed. They are considered active when the corresponding checkbox is.

▸ To activate all three settings, ensure that all three checkboxes are deselected. Click the Execute icon to save the changes.

The Activate BEx History option is a feature that should always be turned on because it assists with query navigation. This function populates the History button that appears when a user opens a workbook or query in the BEx Analyzer or BEx Web. If it is not activated, the History button still appears when opening queries and it will display the message "No Objects Found." This is misleading and frustrating to users that have been in the system multiple times.

When a user executes a query in the BEx Analyzer, there is typically a variable entry screen that allows him the opportunity to prefilter a query by entering characteristic value(s). A query that has optional/mandatory variables will automatically display the Select Values for Variables dialog box (shown in Figure 6.3).

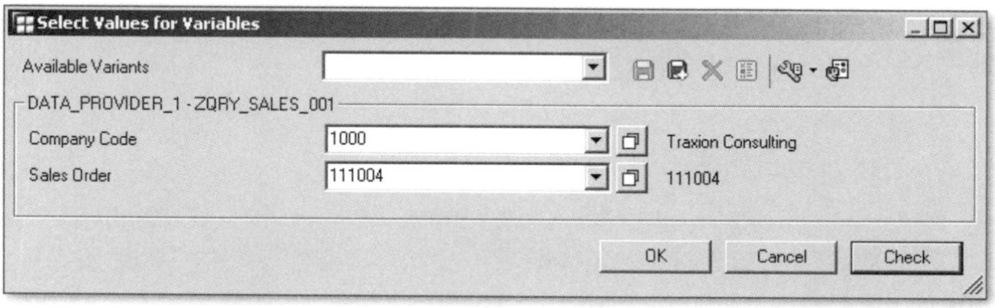

Figure 6.3 Personalization in the BEx Analyzer

Characteristic value variables are typically entered by a user each time the query is executed. Personalization allows a user to store the values for these variables so that they are automatically used each time the query is executed. The dialog box will no longer appear after query personalization has been set. Once a user has entered the relevant variable values they click on the Personalize Variables icon (Figure 6.4).

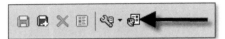

Figure 6.4   Personalize Variables Icon in the Variables Dialog Box

A Personalize Variables window will pop up and allow a user to transfer the assigned variables values to the Personalized Variables section. The desired variables are added to the selection on the right, as displayed in Figure 6.5. Click OK to finish the assignment.

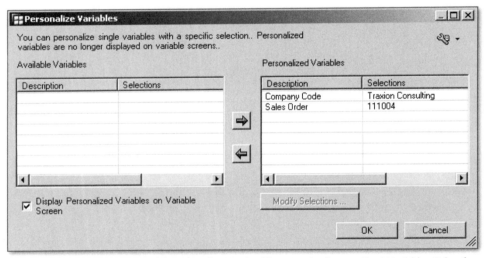

Figure 6.5   Personalizing Variable Values by Moving Them to the Personalized Variables Side of the Window

Variable personalization works the same in a web browser, however, the interface is slightly different. A screenshot of the Web Variable Entry screen is shown in Figure 6.6. The current selection for variable values is displayed in the General Variables table of the Variable Entry screen. Transferring values (using the arrows) from General Variables to the Personalized Variables table completes the assignment.

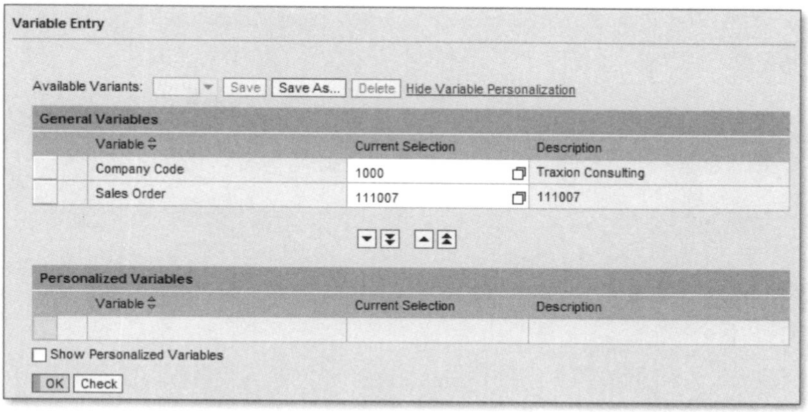

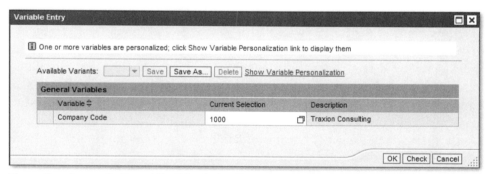

Figure 6.6 Web Personalization of Variable Values

Variables that become personalized are removed from the Variable Entry window the next time a query is executed. An information message will inform users that one or more variables have been personalized. The example shown in Figure 6.7 only shows the variable entry for Company Code as the Sales Order value 111007 has been personalized. Clicking on the Show Variable Personalization link will display personalized variables and allow changes to be made.

Figure 6.7 Personalization of the Sales Order Characteristic Variable

6.3 Analysis Process Designer (APD)

The APD is a relatively little-known tool that is integrated into the Data Warehousing workbench. The Data Warehousing workbench is accessed via Transaction code RSA1. A toolbar icon allows direct access to the APD. Alternatively the menu path EDIT • ANALYSIS PROCESS DESIGNER can be used as well. The layout of the APD is shown in Figure 6.8.

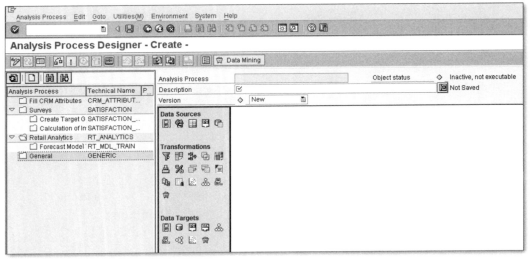

Figure 6.8 The Analysis Process Designer

The graphical user interface (GUI) for the APD allows developers to create, execute, and monitor data transformations that result in additional information or interpretations of the inputs. Data that is already stored in the Data Warehouse (DW) (typically in an InfoProvider, such as a DSO) can be merged, transformed, or extended to derive new calculations from a variety of sources. The resulting calculations are then stored back to a downstream InfoProvider to be used in reporting applications. This closed-loop scenario allows for an analysis process to be modelled by dragging and dropping one or more data sources, defining a data transformation, and finally, choosing a data target to store the results in. Some examples of data transformations available include:

- Joins
- Filter
- Formulas
- Sort
- ABAP Routine
- ABC Classification

▶ Regression Analysis

▶ Prediction with Cluster Model

▶ Weighted Table Scoring

The goal is to attain new insight with the source data being analyzed. The high-level steps required to create and execute a basic analysis process with a data transformation are:

1. Launch the APD from the Data Warehousing workbench

2. Locate a folder under the menu on the left, right-click, and select New.

3. Choose a data source type and drag it to the work area to define its parameters.

4. Select and drag a data transformation into the work area. Enter the necessary parameters.

5. Select and drag a data target type to the work area. Complete any necessary settings in the dialog box.

6. Using the red handles found on each individual node found in the work area, define the overall process flow by dragging and attaching the nodes in the correct order. (See Figure 6.9.)

7. Save the Analysis.

8. Check the process using the Check icon found in the toolbar. Next, activate the process using the Activate icon (next to the Check icon).

9. Execute and monitor the analysis process. Analyze the output data written to the data target.

10. Standard tools such as a job monitor and job logs are available to assist with review and troubleshooting.

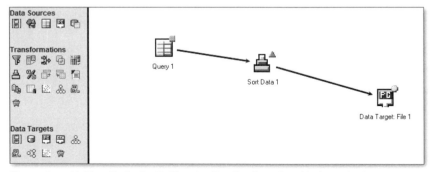

Figure 6.9 Linking Nodes by Pulling the Handles from One Node to the Next

7 Business Objects and SAP Business Warehouse (BW)

The acquisition of Business Objects by SAP should be seen as a positive event for SAP customers. Traditionally, SAP has grown their toolsets organically in buying new tools and modules to augment their Enterprise resource Planning (ERP) and SAP NetWeaver products. Long-term users of SAP BW should remember that Crystal Reports (part of the Business Objects toolset) has enjoyed native integration to SAP BW for many years. This familiarity with each other's product sets in Business Intelligence (BI) has resulted in a roadmap that was presented by SAP's NetWeaver BI product management team in February 2008. This roadmap presented a Business Intelligence Platform (BIP) that selected the tool of choice, or a hybrid of tools, that will be supported and further developed for each of the major categories of Query, Reporting, and Analysis tools. These four categories will be referred to as Enterprise Reporting, Online Analytical Processing (OLAP) Analysis, Dashboarding and Data Quality/Master Data Management.

7.1 SAP Business Objects Roadmap

The product suites from both Business Objects and SAP NetWeaver BI were compared and a decision was made on how to consolidate these competing technologies into a superset of capabilities that will benefit BI users in the future. This merged tool set will be available in two configurations: base and premium. The premium offering will offer more robust versions of each tool and have additional features available, but will come with an additional cost.

In the Enterprise Reporting space, Business Objects has the best product. Crystal Reports is a pervasive tool that is much richer in functionality when compared to the relatively new BEx Report Designer tool that shipped with SAP NetWeaver BI 7.0. As a result, Crystal Reports has become the standard in this space. Crystal Reports Light will ship with the base offering while a full version of Crystal Reports will ship with the premium offering. The BEx Report Designer will not be developed further; however, it should be supported through 2016 (based on the BIP roadmap).

The OLAP analysis category consists of the Business Explorer (BEx) Web Analyzer, BEx Excel Analyzer, and Business Objects Voyager. These tools provide an ad hoc analysis environment for slicing and dicing data into different views. A superset of these three tools will be created into a new product codenamed Pioneer. The Web Analyzer will not be enhanced further; however, the BEx Analyzer that is integrated with Microsoft Excel will survive as a component of Pioneer.

The Dashboarding category consists of the BEx Web Application Designer (WAD) from SAP and Xcelsius and the DashboardBuilder from Business Objects. These products are merging together to create a new tool called Xcelsius+, which will establish itself as the flagship product for dashboarding. Xcelsius has always impressed since Business Objects acquired it a few years ago. It certainly adds additional value to the overall product set going forward. Like the Web Analyzer, the BEx WAD will not receive any future enhancements.

The Master Data Management (MDM) product from SAP will be the cornerstone for data quality and data cleansing functions. Business Objects Data Quality (DQ) offering will flow into the MDM tool. This integration between DQ and MDM will be the focus of development and an enhanced version of MDM, coined MDM+ in the BIP roadmap, will be available by 2010. Business Objects customers should know that DQ will continue to be offered as a standalone tool.

A summary of the base and premium offerings being developed through 2010 is depicted in Figure 7.1. By 2016, support for the BEx tools no longer being enhanced will end. The best approach for SAP customers is to consider each of the Business Objects tools individually and to bring these tools into the fold in a phased approach that provides them with enough time to understand the benefits while providing users with time to learn how to interact with the new tools. One clear option is to switch from the BEx Report Designer to Crystal Reports Light. Not only is Crystal Reports Lite a better tool for Enterprise Reporting, it's also quite likely that many SAP users have more experience with it than the BEx Report Designer. This hybrid approach is likely the best strategy for SAP customers who do not have a compelling reason or immediate need to upgrade to the premium offering. This approach also allows some breathing room for the SAP Business Objects division to tighten up the integration and resolve any issues without a customer having to deal with them early on.

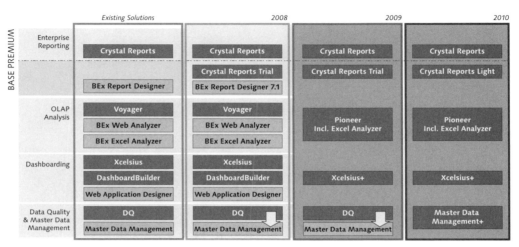

Figure 7.1   BI Platform Roadmap through 2010. Source: SAP BIP Roadmap – Short Version

7.2   The Return of BW

The merger with Business Objects has again resulted in a shift in naming conventions by SAP for the core SAP NetWeaver BI product set. Formally, SAP has rebranded Business Objects as SAP Business Objects and has added SAP Business Objects as a portfolio area at www.sap.com. The Business Objects website will be shutting down.

BW is back. The term SAP NetWeaver BI is replaced with SAP NetWeaver BW. BI will be associated only with the tools and products available from the SAP Business Objects portfolio.

The table below will assist with the 2009 vocabulary change by showing the old and new terminology associated with each name change.

Old Terminology	New Terminology
Business Objects — an SAP Company	SAP Business Objects
www.businessobjects.com	*www.sap.com*
SAP NetWeaver BI	SAP NetWeaver BW
BEx Tools	SAP BEx
SAP NetWeaver BI Accelerator	SAP NetWeaver BW Accelerator
Business Objects	SAP Business Objects

Table 7.1   Summary of SAP and SAP Business Objects Name Changes

Appendices

A   Glossary

Aggregate Stores the dataset of an In-foCube redundantly and persistently in a summarized form on the database, thereby resulting in improved performance.

BEx Broadcaster A tool for precalculating and distributing Web templates, queries, query views, reports, and workbooks. Precalculated objects and online links can be broadcasted. Broadcast settings can be created using a Wizard that provides step-by-step instructions.

BEx Query Designer A tool for defining queries that are based on a selection of InfoObjects. By inserting a combination of characteristics and key figures, you define how the data is evaluated and presented in the query results set.

BEx Web Application Designer (WAD) Desktop application for creating graphical BI cockpits using HTML pages that leverage SAP BI content as an additional element. Requires no programming knowledge but allows direct access to HTML, if required.

Business Explorer (BEx) Refers to the suite of analytical and reporting tools available within SAP BI.

Business Explorer Analyzer Analytical, reporting, and design tool of the BEx suite that is embedded in Microsoft Excel. Typically used to analyze and plan data using a previously created query. Drag-and-drop functionality and a context menu allow users to filter, drill down, and sort data as required.

As of version 7.0, the BEx Analyzer includes a design mode and an analysis mode.

Business Explorer Browser A tool for categorizing and managing SAP BW workbooks, queries, and external documents that functions as an SAP BW desktop. This legacy application is only available with version BW 3.x or earlier.

Cascading Style Sheets (CSS) A style sheet language that describes the presentation of a document written in a markup language. Its most common application is to style web pages written in HTML and XHTML.

Crystal Reports Report definition created using the Crystal Reports Designer. Crystal Reports are designed for presenting quality reports, so there are many options for enhanced formatting. Reports can vary from simple tables to layouts featuring charts, cross-tabs, and nested subreports.

Data Store Object (DSO) An object consisting of three transparent, flat tables (activation queue, active data, and change log) that allow for detailed data storage.

Data Warehouse (DW) A repository of electronically stored data. In most cases it's a collection of data created by integrating datasets from one or more source systems. The means to extract, retrieve, and analyze data; transform and load data; and to manage a data dictionary are also considered essential components of a data-warehousing system. The goal of a data warehouse is to transform data into information that is readily available to users in a timely fashion.

Data Warehousing Workbench (DWB)   The central tool for creating data-warehousing processes and objects. It allows for data modeling and has tools to control, monitor, and maintain processes involved in the administration of an SAP BI system.

Dimension   A grouping of characteristics that logically belong together. Dimensions are used to organize data within applications based on the type of information involved.

Extraction, Transformation, Loading (ETL)   The way in which data actually gets loaded into a Data Warehouse. It's the process of migrating source data from Enterprise Resource Planning (ERP) software or other typical transactional systems to a data-warehouse database.

Information Broadcasting   Information is distributed by using the BEx Broadcaster or the Broadcasting Wizard available with SAP BI. Users can precalculate queries, query views, Web templates, reports, or workbooks and broadcast them by email, to a portal, or to a printer. Output formats include HTML, ZIP, PDF, and online links.

Navigation Block   Item that retrieves data from a query view and displays it in the form of a table. All characteristics and key figures of the query view are listed in the table, and their filter values are displayed. You can interact with the navigational block to update the results or to add/remove additional filters.

InfoArea   A set of logically grouped data targets or InfoProviders grouped together in a hierarchy. The relationship of InfoAreas to InfoCubes in BI resembles the relationship of directories to files in a Windows operating system.

InfoCube   A quantity of relational tables linked according to a star schema that consists of a fact table with several dimension tables.

InfoObject   Business objects (e.g., customers or sales) that can be sub-divided into characteristics, key figures, units, and time or technical characteristics.

InfoProvider   Objects for which queries in SAP BI can be created or executed against. Includes DSO objects, InfoCubes, InfoSets, Master Data, and MultiCubes/MultiProviders.

Metadata   Commonly referred to as "data about data." Metadata describes the origin, history, and other attributes of data.

MultiCube   Also called a MultiProvider. Logically joins data from several basic InfoProviders (InfoCubes, DSO, etc.) together. MultiCubes themselves contain no actual data records, which come exclusively from the underlying Basic InfoCubes.

MultiProvider   Type of InfoProvider that combines data from several InfoProviders, making it available for reporting. The actual MultiProvider contains no data.

Online Analytical Processing (OLAP)   Quickly provides answers to analytical queries that are dimensional in nature. OLAP is part of the broader category of business intelligence, which also encompasses relational reporting. The typical applications of OLAP are in business reporting for sales, marketing, management reporting, financial reporting, and similar areas. The term OLAP was created as a slight modification of the traditional database term OLTP (Online Transaction Processing).

Presentation Layer   An SAP BI layer that consists of the BEx tools that allow a user to retrieve data and format it as they choose.

Reporting Agent   Tool for scheduling reporting functions in the background. Includes functions such as precalculating Web templates, printing queries, managing bookmarks, and evaluating exception-based reporting.

Results Area   Part of a BEx Analyzer workbook or a Web Report that displays the results of a query in a tabular format.

Scheduling Package   Logical collection of several reporting agent settings assigned together for background processing.

Web Application Designer (WAD)   A desktop tool through which Web applications can be created. It is similar to Web authoring tools Microsoft Frontpage and Adobe Dreamweaver. You can use the BEx Web Application Designer to create Web applications and to generate HTML pages that contain BI-specific placeholders such as tables, charts, radio buttons, or maps. These objects, which retrieve BI data from a data provider and place it in a Web application as HTML, are known as Web items.

Web Item   Object that retrieves data from a data provider and presents it as HTML in a Web application.

Web Template   An HTML document that determines the structure of a Web application. It contains placeholders for SAP BI items along with standard Web content. Standard Web templates are predelivered with SAP BI. The standard templates can be modified for various business usage scenarios or new templates can be developed from scratch.

Workbook   A file containing several worksheets. SAP BI queries are embedded into worksheets and can be interacted with using the Business Explorer Analyzer tool. Workbooks can be saved to public roles or saved to a private favorites folder.

B   The Author

Peter Scott, Director – SAP BI Practice, Traxion Consulting, Inc., has over nine years of Business Intelligence experience with a mastery level in SAP BI reporting, SAP BI Project Management and Enterprise Information Strategy. He has directed over a dozen project lifecycles as a Project Manager, Architect and Lead. Peter's consultancy work with companies across North America has included designing corporate management reporting strategies and delivering a wide range of custom training workshops, executive dashboards, and producing enterprise-wide reporting applications. He advises clients on deploying Business Intelligence across their organization and helps customers understand and leverage the new capabilities available from SAP Business Objects.

Peter holds a B.Sc. in Computer Science, a B.Sc. in Biology/Genetics, has an MBA from Queen's University and is a Certified Management Accountant. He speaks regularly at BI events and is authoring his second book for SAP PRESS on BI Reporting, due out in May 2009.

Traxion Consulting is an industry leader in implementing business intelligence solutions that enable organizations to more efficiently analyze their data and thus make better business decisions. Traxion is 100% focused on providing services and solutions to SAP customers across North America. *www.traxionconsulting.com.*

Index

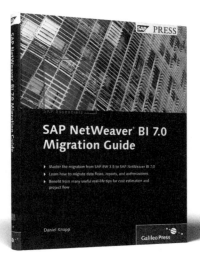

Master the functional professional migration of SAP BW 3.5 to SAP NetWeaver BI 7.0

Find out how to migrate data flows, reports, and authorizations

Use the many valuable tips from real-life projects on effort estimating and project progression

Daniel Knapp

SAP NetWeaver BI 7.0 Migration Guide

SAP PRESS Essentials 50

SAP NetWeaver BI 7.0 includes major changes from earlier releases, making migrations a challenging task, but with this book, consultants, developers, power users, and project teams will find the knowledge needed for technical and functional NetWeaver BI 7.0 migrations. Using real-life examples and highlighting SAP-recommended approaches, you'll work through data, authorizations, report migration and more. Both the automatic and manual aspects of report migration are highlighted, with particular attention to the radically revised Web reporting.

181 pp., 2008, 68,– Euro / US$ 85
ISBN 978-1-59229-228-8

>> www.sap-press.de/1852

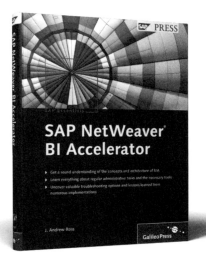

Get a sound understanding of the business impact and technical architecture of BI accelerator

Learn all you need to know about basic and advanced administrative tasks and the available tools

Benefit from technical background information and experience gained via numerous implementations

J. Andrew Ross

SAP NetWeaver BI Accelerator

This SAP PRESS Essentials book is your A-to-Z guide to understanding, setting up, and operating the SAP NetWeaver BI Accelerator. After explaining the concept behind and the architecture of the BI Accelerator, the author provides detailed advice on all administrative tasks such as: setting up the RFC connection, building and maintaining the indexes, cloning the software onto new blades, updating the TREX engine, and much more. A substantial chapter is dedicated to troubleshooting and should boost your confidence when repairing the RFC connection, reorganizing the index landscape, checking and rebuilding indexes, or creating traces to send to SAP Service engineers. A final chapter looks at future developments and success stories, and a glossary enables you to check specialist terms effortlessly.

260 pp., 2009, 68,– Euro / US$ 85.00, ISBN 978-1-59229-192-2

>> www.sap-press.de/1719

Provides a complete end-to-end overview of the BusinessObjects integration

Teaches you how to set up your NetWeaver 7.0 system for using Crystal Reports, Xcelsius, Web Intelligence, and more BO tools

Includes best practices for portal integration, security, and troubleshooting

Ingo Hilgefort

Integrating SAP BusinessObjects XI 3.1 Tools with SAP NetWeaver

This book is about the integration of BusinessObjects BI tools (release XI 3.1) with SAP NetWeaver 7.0 and SAP ERP 6.0 landscapes. If you are a BI administrator, technical consultant, or implementation project lead: You will learn about the actual installation and configuration of the software in combination with the SAP system and will be able to use the BusinessObjects BI tools for creating reports and analytics. You will get started with the BusinessObjects software but will also understand how the SAP NetWeaver BW concepts are being mapped to BusinessObjects software.

approx. 258 pp., 68,– Euro / US$ 85.00
ISBN 978-1-59229-274-5, May 2009

>> www.sap-press.de/2053

Interested in reading more?

Please visit our Web site for all
new book releases from SAP PRESS.

www.sap-press.com